TAPESTRY

JOURNEYS TO CULTURAL UNDERSTANDING

TAPESTRY

The **Tapestry** program of language materials is based on the concepts presented in *The Tapestry of Language Learning: The Individual in the Communicative Classroom* by Robin C. Scarcella & Rebecca L. Oxford.

❖

Each title in this program focuses on:

❖

Individual learner strategies and instruction

❖

The relatedness of skills

❖

Ongoing self-assessment

❖

Authentic material as input

❖

Theme-based learning linked to task-based instruction

❖

Attention to all aspects of communicative competence

JOURNEYS TO CULTURAL UNDERSTANDING

Debra Chan

Judith Kaplan-Weinger

Deborah Sandstrom

Heinle & Heinle Publishers
An International Thomson
Publishing Company
Boston, Massachusetts, 02116, USA

I T P

The publication of *Journeys to Cultural Understanding* was directed by the members of the Heinle & Heinle Global Innovations Publishing Team:

Elizabeth Holthaus: Global Innovations Team Leader
David C. Lee, Editorial Director
John F. McHugh, Market Development Director
Lisa McLaughlin, Production Editor

Also participating in the publication of this program were:

Publisher: Stanley J. Galek
Assistant Editor: Kenneth Mattsson
Manufacturing Coordinator: Mary Beth Hennebury
Full Service Project Manager/Compositor: PC&F, Inc.
Interior Design: Maureen Lauran
Cover Design: Maureen Lauran

Manufactured in the United States of America

ISBN: 0-8384-3959-4

Heinle & Heinle Publishers is an International Thomson Publishing Company.

10 9 8 7 6 5 4 3 2 1

To Suzanne Leibman—a perfect mentor, a true friend whose laughter and nurturing make my journey possible.

DC

To my husband, Larry, and my children, Sarah, Jacob, and Tyler, and to my parents, Evelyn and Milton Kaplan—endless support, endless love from you to me to you. And to Eduarda, for all you know and all you share.

JKW

To Carmen Tolhurst with gratitude for leading me into this field and providing a guiding light during my first years of ESL, and to my husband, John, long suffering yet still supportive.

DS

PHOTO CREDITS

1, Courtesy of NASA; 2, © 1992 Claudia Kunin/Tony Stone Worldwide; 5 top, © 1989 Ulrike Welsch/PhotoEdit; 5 bottom, © Joe Carini/The Image Works; 15, © Carrie Boretz/The Image Works; 16, © Owen Franken/Stock, Boston; 25, © Bruce Forster/All Stock; 37, © Jean Marc Giboux/Gamma-Liaison; 41, © Tony Freeman/PhotoEdit; 42, © 1989 P. McCarten/PhotoEdit; 44, © Don and Pat Valenti/Tony Stone Images, Inc.; 46, © 1989 Owen Franken/Stock, Boston; 49, © 1990 Spencer Grant/Stock, Boston; 55, Les Smith/FPG; 59, Steve and Mary Skjold/PhotoEdit; 62 left, © David Young-Wolff/PhotoEdit; 62 right, © 1992 Mike Powell/Tony Stone Images; 66 top, © Bohdan Hrynewych/Stock, Boston; 66 bottom left, © Tony Freeman/PhotoEdit; 66 bottom right, © Bill Aron Photography/PhotoEdit, 71, © Don Smetzer/Tony Stone Worldwide; 76, FPG; 80, C. Granitsas/The Image Works; 82, © Michael Newman/PhotoEdit; 89. © 1989, John Turner/FPG; 92, © John Waterman/Tony Stone Worldwide; 94, © Michael Weisbrot and Family/Stock, Boston; 107, © Jerry Berndt, Stock, Boston; 109, © B. Bachmann/The Image Works; 119, © R. Sidney/The Image Works; 121, Tony Stone Worldwide; 135, © Joseph Nettis/Tony Stone Worldwide; 139, © Amy C. Etra/PhotoEdit; 148, McKiernan/Gamma Liaison; 155, © Ric Ergenbright/AllStock; 165, © Jim Pickerell/Gamma Liaison; 169, © Paul Harris/AllStock; 170, © Rolf Adlercreutz/Gamma Liaison.

TEXT ACKNOWLEDGMENTS

16, "Wrong-Way Pedestrians Irksome Too," Chicago Tribune, January 25, 1993 by Gary Washburn. © Copyrighted January 15, 1993, Chicago Tribune Company. All rights reserved. Used with permission.

22, Reprinted with permission of the *East-West Church and Ministry Report.*

26, Excerpt from TILL WE HAVE FACES, A MYTH RETOLD. Copyright © 1957, 1956 by C.S. Lewis and renewed 1985, 1984 by Arthur Owen Barfield, reprinted by permission of Harcourt Brace & Company.

31, Material from "You Have Left Your Lotus Pods on the Bus." Copyright © 1979 by Paul Bowles. Reprinted from *Collected Stories of Paul Bowles* with the permission of Black Sparrow Press.

37, Copyright © 1990 by Amy Tan. Reprinted by permission of Amy Tan and the Sandra Dijkstra Literary Agency.

42, Excerpt from IMAGINING AMERICA by Sharon Sloan Fiffer. Reprinted by permission from Paragon House.

70, "The Cave" by Glenn W. Dresbach. From COLLECTED POEMS by Glenn Ward Dresbach. The Caxton Printers, Ltd. Caldwell, Idaho 83605

72, From FODOR'S INDIAN AMERICA by Fodor's Travel Publications, Inc. Copyright © 1975 by Fodor's Travel Publications, Inc. Reprinted by permission of the publisher.

73, From *Leaves of Grass* by Walt Whitman, Bantam Doubleday Dell Publishing Group, Inc.

76, From FODOR'S INDIAN AMERICA by Fodor's Travel Publications, Inc. Copyright © 1975 by Fodor's Travel Publications, Inc. Reprinted by permission of the publisher.

77, Letter to the Editor by Amy Wu. Reprinted by permission of MS. Magazine, © 1992.

81, From LIVING OUT LOUD by Anna Quindlen, © 1988, Ballatine Books, Inc.

95, Excerpt from "Empathy Can Span the Abyss." Reprinted with permission from MODERN MATURITY and author Malcolm Boyd. Copyright 1992, American Association of Retired Persons.

98, "See Jack . . . teach kindergarten?" by Cindy Schreuder. Copyrighted October 9, 1992, Chicago Tribune Company, all rights reserved, used with permission.

108, Excerpt from WHEN YOU LOOK LIKE YOUR PASSPORT, IT'S TIME TO GO HOME by Erma Bombeck, copyright © 1991 by Erma Bombeck. Reprinted by permission of Harper Collins Publishers Inc.

112, "For U.S. immigrants, accent is on sounding like everyone else" by Leu Siew Ying. © Copyrighted October 30, 1991, Chicago Tribune Company, all rights reserved, used with permission.

115, Reprinted by permission of Sterling Lord Literistic, Inc.

118, "Ad Firm Tries to Crack the Code of Teenspeak" by Andrew Hermann. Reprinted with permission from the *Chicago Sun-Times,* © 1993.

128, Reprinted by permission of International Creative Management, Inc. Copyright 1991 by Deborah Tannen. Taken from the author's bestselling book, YOU JUST DON'T UNDERSTAND.

158, Reprinted by permission of the publishers and the Trustees of Amherst College from THE POEMS OF EMILY DICKENSON, Thomas H. Johnson, ed., Cambridge, Mass.: The Belknap Press of Harvard University Press, Copyright © 1951, 1955, 1979, 1983 by the President and Fellows of Harvard College.

173–176, The *Culturgram* for Russia is reprinted with the permission of Brigham Young University's David M. Kennedy Center for International Studies. *Culturgrams* are available for over 110 areas. For ordering information or a free catalog, please call 1-800-528-6279.

WELCOME TO TAPESTRY

*E*nter the world of Tapestry! Language learning can be seen as an ever-developing tapestry woven with many threads and colors. The elements of the tapestry are related to different language skills like listening and speaking, reading and writing; the characteristics of the teachers; the desires, needs, and backgrounds of the students; and the general second language development process. When all these elements are working together harmoniously, the result is a colorful, continuously growing tapestry of language competence of which the student and the teacher can be proud.

This volume is part of the Tapestry program for students of English as a second language (ESL) at levels from beginning to "bridge" (which follows the advanced level and prepares students to enter regular postsecondary programs along with native English speakers). Tapestry levels include:

Beginning
Low Intermediate
High Intermediate
Low Advanced
High Advanced
Bridge

Because the Tapestry Program provides a unified theoretical and pedagogical foundation for all its components, you can optimally use all the Tapestry student books in a coordinated fashion as an entire curriculum of materials. (They will be published from 1993 to 1996 with further editions likely thereafter.) Alternatively, you can decide to use just certain Tapestry volumes, depending on your specific needs.

Tapestry is primarily designed for ESL students at postsecondary institutions in North America. Some want to learn ESL for academic or career advancement, others for social and personal reasons. Tapestry builds directly on all these motivations. Tapestry stimulates learners to do their best. It enables learners to use English naturally and to develop fluency as well as accuracy.

Tapestry Principles

The following principles underlie the instruction provided in all of the components of the Tapestry program.

EMPOWERING LEARNERS

Language learners in Tapestry classrooms are active and increasingly responsible for developing their English language skills and related cultural abilities. This self direction leads to better, more rapid learning. Some cultures virtually train their students to be passive in the classroom, but Tapestry weans them from passivity by providing exceptionally high interest materials, colorful and motivating activities, personalized self-reflection tasks, peer tutoring and other forms of cooperative learning, and powerful learning strategies to boost self direction in learning.

The empowerment of learners creates refreshing new roles for teachers, too. The teacher serves as facilitator, co-communicator, diagnostician, guide, and helper. Teachers are set free to be more creative at the same time their students become more autonomous learners.

HELPING STUDENTS IMPROVE THEIR LEARNING STRATEGIES

Learning strategies are the behaviors or steps an individual uses to enhance his or her learning. Examples are taking notes, practicing, finding a conversation partner, analyzing words, using background knowledge, and controlling anxiety. Hundreds of such strategies have been identified. Successful language learners use language learning strategies that are most effective for them given their particular learning style, and they put them together smoothly to fit the needs of a given language task. On the other hand, the learning strategies of less successful learners are a desperate grab-bag of ill-matched techniques.

All learners need to know a wide range of learning strategies. All learners need systematic practice in choosing and applying strategies that are relevant for various learning needs. Tapestry is one of the only ESL programs that overtly weaves a comprehensive set of learning strategies into language activities in all its volumes. These learning strategies are arranged in eight broad categories throughout the Tapestry books:

Forming concepts
Personalizing
Remembering new material
Managing your learning
Understanding and using emotions
Overcoming limitations
Testing Hypotheses
Learning with Others

The most useful strategies are sometimes repeated and flagged with a note, "It Works! Learning Strategy . . ." to remind students to use a learning strategy they have already encountered. This recycling reinforces the value of learning strategies and provides greater practice.

RECOGNIZING AND HANDLING LEARNING STYLES EFFECTIVELY

Learners have different learning styles (for instance, visual, auditory, hands- on; reflective, impulsive; analytic, global; extroverted, introverted; closure-oriented, open). Particularly in an ESL setting, where students come from vastly different cultural backgrounds, learning styles differences abound and can cause "style conflicts."

Unlike most language instruction materials, Tapestry provides exciting activities specifically tailored to the needs of students with a large range of learning styles. You can use any Tapestry volume with the confidence that the activities and materials are intentionally geared for many different styles. Insights from the latest educational and psychological research undergird this style-nourishing variety.

OFFERING AUTHENTIC, MEANINGFUL COMMUNICATION

Students need to encounter language that provides authentic, meaningful communication. They must be involved in real-life communication tasks that cause them to *want* and *need* to read, write, speak, and listen to English. Moreover, the tasks—to be most effective—must be arranged around themes relevant to learners.

Themes like family relationships, survival in the educational system, personal health, friendships in a new country, political changes, and protection of the environment are all valuable to ESL learners. Tapestry focuses on topics like these. In every Tapestry volume, you will see specific content drawn from very broad areas such as home life, science and technology, business, humanities, social sciences, global issues, and multiculturalism. All the themes are real and important, and they are fashioned into language tasks that students enjoy.

At the advanced level, Tapestry also includes special books each focused on a single broad theme. For instance, there are two books on business English, two on English for science and technology, and two on academic communication and study skills.

UNDERSTANDING AND VALUING DIFFERENT CULTURES

Many ESL books and programs focus completely on the "new" culture, that is, the culture which the students are entering. The implicit message is that ESL students should just learn about this target culture, and there is no need to understand their own culture better or to find out about the cultures of their international classmates. To some ESL students, this makes them feel their own culture is not valued in the new country.

Tapestry is designed to provide a clear and understandable entry into North American culture. Nevertheless, the Tapestry Program values *all* the cultures found in the ESL classroom. Tapestry students have constant opportunities to become "culturally fluent" in North American culture while they are learning English, but they also have the chance to think about the cultures of their classmates and even understand their home culture from different perspectives.

INTEGRATING THE LANGUAGE SKILLS

Communication in a language is not restricted to one skill or another. ESL students are typically expected to learn (to a greater or lesser degree) all four language skills: reading, writing, speaking, and listening. They are also expected to develop strong grammatical competence, as well as becoming socioculturally sensitive and knowing what to do when they encounter a "language barrier."

Research shows that multi-skill learning is more effective than isolated-skill learning, because related activities in several skills provide reinforcement and refresh the learner's memory. Therefore, Tapestry integrates all the skills. A given Tapestry volume might highlight one skill, such as reading, but all other skills are also included to support and strengthen overall language development.

However, many intensive ESL programs are divided into classes labeled according to one skill (Reading Comprehension Class) or at most two skills (Listening/Speaking Class or Oral Communication Class). The volumes in the Tapestry Program can easily be used to fit this traditional format, because each volume clearly identifies its highlighted or central skill(s).

Grammar is interwoven into all Tapestry volumes. However, there is also a separate reference book for students, *The Tapestry Grammar,* and a Grammar Strand composed of grammar "work-out" books at each of the levels in the Tapestry Program.

Other Features of the Tapestry Program

PILOT SITES

It is not enough to provide volumes full of appealing tasks and beautiful pictures. Users deserve to know that the materials have been pilot-tested. In many ESL series, pilot testing takes place at only a few sites or even just in the classroom of the author. In contrast, Heinle & Heinle Publishers have developed a network of Tapestry Pilot Test Sites throughout North America. At this time, there are approximately 40 such sites, although the number grows weekly. These sites try out the materials and provide suggestions for revisions. They are all actively engaged in making Tapestry the best program possible.

AN OVERALL GUIDEBOOK

To offer coherence to the entire Tapestry Program and especially to offer support for teachers who want to understand the principles and practice of Tapestry, we have written a book entitled, *The Tapestry of Language Learning. The Individual in the Communicative Classroom* (Scarcella and Oxford, published in 1992 by Heinle & Heinle).

A Last Word

We are pleased to welcome you to Tapestry! We use the Tapestry principles every day, and we hope these principles—and all the books in the Tapestry Program—provide you the same strength, confidence, and joy that they give us. We look forward to comments from both teachers and students who use any part of the Tapestry Program.

Rebecca L. Oxford
University of Alabama
Tuscaloosa, Alabama

Robin C. Scarcella
University of California at Irvine
Irvine, California

PREFACE

*C*ommunicative approaches to language teaching focus on the learning of language in context—a context that includes both the structures and functions of language. For students of English as a second language who are studying in English-speaking environments, that context is the surrounding English-speaking community. Learning the language must, therefore, include learning the culture.

Louise Damen has defined culture learning as "the fifth dimension in the language classroom." For Damen, culture learning occupies as important a position in the classroom as speaking, listening, reading, and writing. We, too, believe that culture learning is a vital corollary to language learning, so vital that it merits, when possible, a course and text of its own.

There are many ways a text on culture can introduce second-language students to their contact culture—the culture in which they now live. First, a text can offer bits of information about individual cultural groups and the reasons the members of those groups act and believe as they do. Unfortunately, this information is typically far from comprehensive and is often dangerously narrow and stereotypical. A culture text can also offer historical, descriptive summaries of cultural groups and tips for maintaining successful interactions with their members. Again, unfortunately, this information may prepare students to interact with stereotypes rather than individuals. Finally, a culture text can provide students with the tools to acquire cultural information and increase cultural knowledge on their own—and this is the goal of *Journeys to Cultural Understanding.*

A text on cross-cultural understanding for the high-advanced college or university student of English as a second language, *Journeys* can serve as the primary text for classes in both culture learning and conversation. Additionally, *Journeys* is an appropriate supplementary text for classes in reading and writing English. A cassette tape accompanies the text, and an instructor's manual is available. The cassette tape provides audio input for a number of the text activities, and the instructor's manual offers tapescripts of materials on the cassette and suggestions on how to use the varied activities in the text.

To make the study of culture active and participatory, *Journeys* adopts a technique grounded in anthropological theory. Viewing a culture as a group of individuals who behave in systematic and rule-governed ways, *Journeys* involves students in ethnographic observation, interviews, and behavioral analysis. Student tasks focus on discovering the patterns of cultural behavior exhibited by members of their contact culture. To aid this discovery process, students make use of an observational and analytic tool—the BEHAVIOR model—to investigate the behaviors and points of view common to and guided by the expectations of a culture's members.

At the same time, as part of the *Tapestry* curriculum, *Journeys* integrates listening, speaking, reading, and writing tasks. Authentic materials from literature, newspapers, and magazines provide input for these tasks. More significantly, however, students themselves provide input by collecting observational data and cultural artifacts in the course of their ethnographic fieldwork. In individual, small-group, and whole-class activities, students apply learning strategies that are both direct and indirect, cognitive and metacognitive, social and personal. Through the tasks, materials, and strategies incorporated in *Journeys,* students increase their communicative competence as they build their cultural competence.

Thematically, the twelve chapters of *Journeys* are divided into three areas of concentration: Chapters 1 through 4 introduce students to the concept of culture and its role in their lives; Chapters 5 through 10 examine individually some of the more prominent components of culture; and Chapter 11 explores the beliefs, viewpoints, and ideals revealed through the behaviors of the members of a culture. The final chapter, 12, presents the journey to cultural understanding as an excursion without end.

Chapter 1—Cultural Awareness—explores the meaning of culture and its role in one's life. Chapter 2—Crossing Cultures—highlights the components of the process of cultural adjustment: expectations, similarities, differences, and struggles. Chapter 3—Understanding Worldview—concentrates students' attention on the role of worldview in developing cultural awareness and easing cultural adjustment. Chapter 4—Observing Culture—completes the introduction to culture by presenting and engaging students in the use of the ethnographic BEHAVIOR model for observing and analyzing the patterns and systems of cultural behavior.

Chapter 5—The Places of Culture—focuses on the role and meaning of places to individuals and their culture. Chapter 6—The People of Culture— investigates the relationship between a culture and its people and illustrates how diversity exists in the presence of a united people. Chapter 6 also introduces interviewing as another ethnographic technique for acquiring cultural knowledge. In Chapter 7—The Society of Culture—students extend their investigation of the people of a culture by examining how the culture is structured and defined by the social institutions of family, age, and gender. The relationship between language and culture is the focus of Chapters 8 and 9. Chapter 8—The Language of Culture—examines this relationship as it is revealed in sounds and words. In turn, Chapter 9—The Culture of Language—examines this relationship as it is revealed in the power of language to identify roles and influence behavior. Influence is also a major theme of Chapter 10—The Channels of Culture—which examines the role of the print, broadcast, and advertising media in shaping and reflecting culture.

The final theme of *Journeys* explores the meaning of culture. Chapter 11— Cultural Values—explores the beliefs, viewpoints, and ideals revealed through the behaviors engaged in by a culture's members. In the culminating chapter, Chapter 12—Your Journey Continues—students review what they have learned about cultural investigation, about culture as a concept, and about their native and contact cultures. Finally, students consider what they would like to learn in the next stages of their journey.

Each chapter of *Journeys* integrates a variety of task types as well as language skills and learning strategies. Among the tasks students encounter are the following:

TASK CHART		
TITLE	**TYPE**	**PURPOSE**
Introductory Text	individual/ class	introduces chapter theme
Consider This	individual	used at beginning of each chapter to engage students in the chapter theme
		used within chapters to encourage reflection on specific concepts
Talk It Over	class	engages students in discussion following a task
Share Your Experience	pair/small group	used to generate reflection on personal experience
Contribute Your Ideas	pair/small group	used to debrief a task or to focus learning
Observation Task	individual/pair	used as the ethnographic focus in chapters 4–12
		involves students in observing naturally occurring behavior or conducting interviews
Listening	individual/small group	provides, on cassette, authentic listening materials and activities related to chapter theme
Reading	individual	provides authentic reading materials related to chapter theme
Language Focus	individual/pair/ small group/ class	pre- and post-listening and reading activities focus on prediction, inference, comprehension, and vocabulary development
Write About It	individual	allows students to generate in-class writings
Assorted Tasks	individual/pair/ small group	includes games, puzzles, dramatizations, and drawings
Checkpoint	individual	provides brief self-assessment summaries of key points
Journal	individual	provides written self-assessment tasks
		encourages written interaction with chapter content or comparison of native and contact culture
The Journey Continues	individual	end-of-chapter readings that review the current chapter and introduce the following chapter

Because *Journeys* is a task-based culture text, it enables students to acquire their knowledge and skills actively. Students increase their understanding of culture by observing and participating in their contact culture. They also call upon their experience as members of their native cultures.

Journeys reminds students that the goal of the language learner may not always be to assimilate into the second culture. They are free to choose, consciously or not, to retain their native culture as their primary or sole culture. Whatever their goals, students can benefit from knowledge of a second culture and the tools for investigating it. By adopting an ethnographic approach to cultural understanding, students learn not only about their second culture but about their native culture as well. Rather than coming away from this text knowing only what members of their contact culture do, students learn how to observe and analyze for themselves what the members of *any* culture do. This ability to investigate a second culture and then to use the collected data for descriptive and comparative analysis of cultural knowledge, values, and behavior is central to becoming culturally competent.

Everyone knows how to behave in at least one culture. Appreciating that all cultures can be investigated in the same way and that such investigation allows us to see both the similarities and differences that exist across cultures is, perhaps, the most valuable knowledge we can share with our ESL students as they engage not only in language learning but also in culture learning. Yet the primary value of *Journey*s is that it not only teaches students about their contact culture but it teaches them how to learn about *any* culture. We hope their successful trip through this text encourages further cultural journeys.

Acknowledgments

With appreciation and gratitude, we acknowledge the contributions to this text of Tapestry editors, Rebecca Oxford and Robin Scarcella; editorial director, David Lee; assistant editor, Kenneth Mattsson; developmental editor, Amy Jamison; and from PC&F, project manager, Elaine Hall; and copyeditor Shirley Simmons.

Additionally, we wish to thank the following reviewers who incorporated this text into their teaching and provided comments on its content and structure: Allison Howe (Harvard University); Jeffra Flaitz (University of South Florida); Laura Le Drean (University of Houston—Downtown); Sally Gearhart (Santa Rosa Junior College); and Jacinta Thomas (College of Lake County, Illinois).

Special acknowledgment and thanks to Suzanne Leibman (College of Lake County) who not only served as a reviewer of this text but also provided endless interest and support.

We acknowledge, too, the contributions of our students, colleagues, and friends, especially Patti and Greg Erickson, Susan Sandstrom, Magaly Dean, Diane Pawelek, and Pamela Solon. Whether providing recollections of cultural experiences, ideas about activity content and structure, or encouragement and enthusiasm for our work, they inspired us and made our goal seem both important and possible.

Finally, we acknowledge the contribution of Lois Rosenberg, with us for the conception and development of this text and always in our thoughts. We thank you for your friendship and for sharing in this endeavor.

Debra Chan
Judith Kaplan-Weinger
Deborah Sandstrom

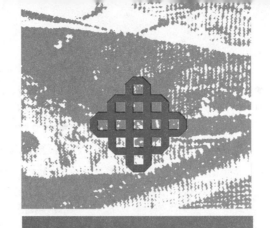

CONTENTS

1 Cultural Awareness   1

INTRODUCTION   2
1.1 WHAT IS CULTURE?   3
1.2 KNOWING YOUR NATIVE CULTURE   4
1.3 GETTING TO KNOW YOUR CONTACT CULTURE   7
1.4 COMPARING CULTURAL BEHAVIORS   9
1.5 REFLECTING ON WHAT YOU HAVE LEARNED   13

2 Crossing Cultures   15

INTRODUCTION   16
2.1 CROSS-CULTURAL EXPERIENCES   17
2.2 IDENTIFYING CULTURAL STRUGGLES   20
2.3 PERSONALIZING CULTURAL ADJUSTMENT   23
2.4 REFLECTING ON WHAT YOU HAVE LEARNED   24

3 Understanding Worldview   25

INTRODUCTION   26
3.1 DIFFERENT PERSPECTIVES   27
3.2 WHEN WORLDVIEWS COLLIDE   30
3.3 WHEN WORLDVIEWS COLLABORATE   37
3.4 REFLECTING ON WHAT YOU HAVE LEARNED   38

4 Observing Culture   41

INTRODUCTION   42
4.1 INTRODUCING OBSERVATION   43
4.2 THE INGREDIENTS OF BEHAVIOR   45
4.3 PRACTICING OBSERVATION WITH THE BEHAVIOR MODEL   47
4.4 REFINING YOUR OBSERVATION SKILLS   48

4.5 CONDUCTING NATURAL
OBSERVATION 50
4.6 REFLECTING ON WHAT
YOU HAVE LEARNED 53

5 The Places of Culture 55

INTRODUCTION 56

5.1 CAMPUS CULTURE 56
5.2 GATHERING
INFORMATION 60
5.3 ANALYZING CAMPUS
CULTURE 61
5.4 PLACES IN COMMUNITY
CULTURE 65
5.5 OBSERVING PLACES
AND BEHAVIORS IN
THE COMMUNITY 67
5.6 FOCUS ON CULTURAL
RULES 69
5.7 REFLECTING ON WHAT
YOU HAVE LEARNED 70

6 The People of Culture 71

INTRODUCTION 72

6.1 INDIVIDUALS AND
THEIR CULTURE 72
6.2 THE IMPACT OF
STEREOTYPES 75
6.3 CULTURAL DIVERSITY 78
6.4 VOICES OF EXPERIENCE 81
6.5 PRESENTING YOUR
RESEARCH 86
6.6 REFLECTING ON WHAT
YOU HAVE LEARNED 88

7 The Society of Culture 89

INTRODUCTION 90

7.1 THE FAMILY 91
7.2 THE SIGNIFICANCE
OF AGE 94
7.3 GENDER ROLES 97
7.4 VOICES OF EXPERIENCE 102
7.5 REFLECTING ON WHAT
YOU HAVE LEARNED 105

8 The Language of Culture 107

INTRODUCTION 108

8.1 THE ROLE OF LANGUAGE
IN CULTURE 109
8.2 THE SOUNDS WE
PRODUCE 110
8.3 THE ACCENTS WE HEAR 111
8.4 THE WORDS WE USE 114
8.5 REFLECTING ON WHAT
YOU HAVE LEARNED 120

9 The Culture of Language 121

INTRODUCTION 122

9.1 ADDRESS FORMS 123
9.2 LANGUAGE AND GENDER 127
9.3 REFLECTING ON WHAT
YOU HAVE LEARNED 133

10 *The Channels of Culture* 135

INTRODUCTION 136
10.1 NEWSPAPERS 137
10.2 MAGAZINES 143
10.3 TELEVISION 146
10.4 ADVERTISEMENTS AND COMMERCIALS 149
10.5 REFLECTING ON WHAT YOU HAVE LEARNED 153

11 *Cultural Values* 155

INTRODUCTION 156
11.1 BEHAVIOR AND CULTURAL VALUES 157
11.2 PROVERBS: CLUES TO CULTURAL VALUES 159
11.3 FURTHER CLUES: SONGS AND OATHS 162
11.4 CULTURAL VALUES— OBSERVING AND INTERVIEWING 165
11.5 REFLECTING ON WHAT YOU HAVE LEARNED 167

12 *Your Journey Continues* 169

INTRODUCTION 170
12.1 WHERE YOU HAVE BEEN 170
12.2 WHERE YOU WOULD LIKE TO GO 176
12.3 REFLECTING ON WHAT YOU HAVE LEARNED 180

Appendices 181

APPENDIX A 182
APPENDIX B 183

Cultural Awareness

Life is either a daring adventure or nothing.

–Helen Keller

I am from Russia, and as all Russians, when I came to America at first I thought that all Americans were very strange. Why? Because they are really different from us. Their habits, behaviors, manners seem very peculiar to me. I have lived here for four months now. I think I am beginning to better understand the Americans. In fact, I am acting more and more like them myself. I can now sit on the floor in the hall waiting for my next class. Sometimes I don't tuck my shirt into my pants. I spend too much time shopping. My neighbors have told me that I am a crazy driver. But I don't mind these changes and I think that there will be others.

–Vicky

Vicky, an ESL student, describes a few cultural differences between her <u>native culture</u> (Russia) and her <u>contact culture</u> (the United States). Upon entering her contact culture, Vicky immediately thought that "all Americans were very strange because they were different." Over time, however, Vicky seemed to adjust to those differences.

TALK IT OVER

1. Vicky has identified a number of ways she has changed her behavior to act more like Americans. What do you think of these changes? Will they make Vicky more American?
2. Vicky believes that after having lived in the United States for four months, she understands Americans better. How well do you understand your contact culture? How would you describe the people who belong to it? How is your contact culture different from your native culture?
3. What changes have you made since coming to your contact culture? How do you feel about those changes? Do you think there will be others?
4. Do you think all people change when they spend a lot of time in a new culture? Why or why not?

CONSIDER THIS

What personal goals do you have for increasing your awareness and understanding of your contact culture? What would you like to know?

_____

_____

_____

This chapter includes activities that will stimulate your awareness of culture. In this chapter, you will explore your native culture and your contact culture. You will also become familiar with your classmates and the cultures they represent. By the end of this chapter you will have gained greater insight into the role of culture in your life.

1.1 WHAT IS CULTURE?

What comes to your mind when you think of culture? How would you describe or define culture?

_____

_____

_____

_____

LEARNING STRATEGY

Forming Concepts: Making a list of your ideas lets you see the culture as a whole.

Generating Categories of Culture

With a partner, make a list of all the parts of culture you can think of and add them to the list below. If you need more space, use another sheet of paper.

CULTURE		
marriage	_____ _____	_____
education	_____	_____
transportation	_____	_____
religion	_____	_____
food	_____	_____

Threads

In earlier Inughuit culture, no formal wedding ceremony existed. Couples just told their neighbors that they were married.

World Cultures

When you have finished making your list of the parts of culture, share your information with your classmates. Together, decide which categories you think are common to all cultures.

CHECKPOINT

Different cultures have different customs. However, while all cultures may not share the same customs or behaviors, there are many categories of culture that are universal—found in all cultures. All cultures, for example, share the category of "marriage." In other words, every culture has rules about marriage—whom one can and cannot marry, how marriage is celebrated, how the bride and groom should dress. The marriage customs may be different, but the general category of "marriage" is common to all cultures.

LEARNING STRATEGY

Remembering New Material: Visualizing what you have learned helps you recall new material.

PICTURE THIS

Considering all the categories of culture you have generated, can you illustrate these in a picture, a chart, or a diagram? What are the relationships among your categories? How might you "draw" culture?

Working in groups of three or four, create an illustration of culture by drawing a picture, a chart, or a diagram.

LEARNING STRATEGY

Testing Hypotheses: Consulting with your classmates allows you to see how others feel about your ideas.

PRESENT YOUR ILLUSTRATIONS

Present your illustration to the rest of your class. Explain why you chose to illustrate culture in the way you did.

1.2 KNOWING YOUR NATIVE CULTURE

What do you know about your native culture? The following questions may help you to think of your own culture in ways you have never thought of before. Read them and think about how you would explain your answers to a person who may not be familiar with your culture.

What Do You Know About Your Culture?

- How do men and women greet one another in your native culture? (For example, do they shake hands, kiss, hug, or bow?)
- What kinds of jobs do men usually have and what kinds do women usually have? (Is it men or women who are usually taxi drivers, secretaries, nurses, or doctors?)
- When you have a conversation with someone, where do you look? (For example, do you make eye contact, look down, or look away?)
- What kinds of foods are popular? Which kinds of foods mix well together and which do not? (For example, Americans might put mustard but probably not mayonnaise on hot dogs.)
- What smells are good or pleasant and what smells are bad or unpleasant? (For example, many Canadians like the smell of freshly baked bread.)
- Who has primary responsibility for raising children? (Is it parents, older siblings, grandparents, day care centers, or others?)
- What behaviors get children in trouble with their parents, teachers, or authorities? (For example, lying, cheating, stealing, or fighting?)
- What types of discipline or punishment are used when children do something wrong?
- What values or beliefs (for example, respect for the elderly, honesty) are always taught to the children?

Threads

In Malta, "children are respectful and often silent in the presence of their fathers."

World Cultures

Threads

"Gritty perseverance, personal autonomy and independence, and respect for the autonomy of others are central themes in Finnish child training and the Finnish personality."

World Cultures

CONTRIBUTE YOUR IDEAS

After you have read and thought about the questions, discuss your answers with a classmate. In this way, you can inform your classmate about your culture and learn about his or her culture.

TALK IT OVER

1. What cultures (or countries) are your classmates from? What languages do your classmates speak?
2. What similarities and differences exist among your classmates' native cultures in the ways

   - women greet one another?
   - men greet one another?
   - men and women greet one another?
   - older and younger people greet one another?

3. Review your answer to this question: What values or beliefs are always taught to the children in your native culture? What similarities and differences exist among your classmates' cultures, judging by their answers to this question?

LEARNING STRATEGY

Managing Your Learning: Evaluating your progress helps you become a successful learner.

JOURNAL

Describe Your Native Culture

As you discussed the questions above with your classmates, perhaps you became aware of your own culture in ways you never thought about before. Write a journal entry in which you describe your native culture. What did you learn about your native culture from the questions and discussion? You may want to summarize your answers to some of the questions above.

1.3 GETTING TO KNOW YOUR CONTACT CULTURE

Images of Your Contact Culture

When you hear the name of your contact culture, what five images or pictures come to your mind? Write your images in the space below:

1. _____
2. _____
3. _____
4. _____
5. _____

The "Find Someone Who . . ." Game

LEARNING STRATEGY

Understanding and Using Emotions: Identifying with your classmates helps you know yourself better.

OBJECTIVE

The objective of this game is to find classmates who know the cultural trivia in the box that follows. The first person to finish is the winner. Before you begin, read the game rules below.

GAME RULES

1. Walk around your classroom and ask your classmates questions to obtain the information requested in the box. All the information relates to the country you are now in.
2. When you find a person who knows the answer to one of the questions, have that person sign his or her name in the appropriate space.
3. No person should sign your sheet more than twice.
4. You may use your own name on your survey, but only twice.

Read the following sentences and make sure you understand and know how to pronounce them before beginning to play the game.

Find Someone Who . . .

1. _____ knows the next business holiday.
2. _____ knows the name of a best-selling car.
3. _____ can name the most popular food.
4. _____ can sing a song in English.
5. _____ can recognize the National Anthem.
6. _____ can name three kinds of Coke.
7. _____ can name three cartoon characters.
8. _____ can name one popular singing group.
9. _____ can name three professional sports teams.
10. _____ knows where the leader of the country is from.
11. _____ can identify the latitude of your city.
12. _____ can name one minority group.
13. _____ has watched a music video.
14. _____ knows a famous minority group leader.
15. _____ can name five politicians.
16. _____ can name one famous song from the sixties.
17. _____ can name the person on a dollar bill.
18. _____ can name one brand name of jeans.
19. _____ can name one famous poet.
20. _____ can name three actors or actresses.

Threads

From 1820–1989, 55,009,566 immigrants were admitted to the United States.

Whitaker's Almanack

TALK IT OVER

1. What is the importance of knowing trivial information about another culture?
2. Is this the only type of information you need to know to understand a culture?
3. What other information is important?

The activities you have just completed in this chapter acquainted you with cultural trivia. Knowing trivial information about a culture is fun; understanding another culture, however, requires deeper exploration. To be able to interact with other people in their culture, you need to know what they do and why. A good way to begin gathering this knowledge is by comparing your native culture with your contact culture.

LEARNING STRATEGY

Personalizing: Reflecting on behavior in your native culture helps you better understand your contact culture.

SHARE YOUR EXPERIENCE

Being a guest in someone's home can be a very different experience in your contact culture than in your native culture. Read and discuss the following questions with a classmate.

What are the rules in your native culture for being a dinner guest?

- Should you bring a gift for the host?
- What items of clothing should you take off when you enter? When you sit down to eat?
- Should you eat everything that is served? Is it impolite to leave food on your plate or in your bowl?
- How much should you eat? How can you politely express that you are full and can't eat any more?
- Should you offer to help the host or hostess clean up after the meal?
- Should you talk while you eat? What topics can you talk about?
- How long should you stay? When should you leave?
- What is the polite way to leave?

CHECKPOINT

Being a guest in someone's home is an example of a **cultural behavior.** While cultures may share the same behaviors, many cultures have different rules for these behaviors. It might be appropriate in a Japanese home, for example, to take off your shoes when you enter the home. Yet taking off your shoes in some American homes may be inappropriate. The cultural behavior, *being a guest in someone's home,* is practiced in both Japanese and American cultures, but the rules for this behavior may differ.

TALK IT OVER

1. What are the two most important rules for being a guest in someone's home in your native culture?
2. Of the cultures represented by your classmates, which have similar rules?

LEARNING STRATEGY

Overcoming Limitations: Talking about the rules of culture with your classmates prepares you for cultural experiences in your community.

SHARE YOUR EXPERIENCE

Here is a list of cultural behaviors common to many cultures:

- ordering food in a restaurant
- celebrating the birth of a child
- caring for a person who is ill
- asking for directions

Choose one of the preceding behaviors. Discuss the rules for that behavior in your native culture and in your contact culture. Write the rules for your contact culture below.

Name of cultural behavior: _____

Rules for cultural behavior: _____

_____

_____

_____

_____

Testing Hypotheses: Listening to another person's experience helps you evaluate your understanding of a culture.

READING

Read the following description of an American tourist's experience in a Hong Kong restaurant. Can you identify with her feelings?

CULTURAL RULES FOR GETTING A TABLE IN A HONG KONG RESTAURANT

The cultural rules for being seated at a table in a busy restaurant in Hong Kong are different than the cultural rules we have in America. In America, we wait at the door of the restaurant and are seated by the host or hostess after the table is cleared, wiped clean, and reset. In crowded restaurants in Hong Kong, customers wait for a table by standing behind the customers who are seated at the table eating. When the customers finish eating, you can immediately sit down at the table even before the busboy clears it.

When I was visiting Hong Kong, I quickly became aware of the cultural rules for getting a table in a restaurant, and I tried to practice these rules. But, to be honest, when I was standing behind the customers while they were eating, I felt like I was being rude. I felt like I was saying—at least through body language—"Hurry up and finish eating!" I also felt like everyone in the restaurant was staring at me.

Although I understand the appropriate cultural rules for getting a table in Hong Kong, I have a difficult time practicing these rules.

–Nancy

TALK IT OVER

1. The cultural behavior that Nancy describes is "getting a seat in a restaurant." How do the cultural rules for this behavior in Hong Kong differ from the rules in your contact culture?
2. Why did Nancy have a difficult time practicing the Hong Kong rules?
3. Do you think Nancy should obey the Hong Kong rules while she is in Hong Kong? Or do you think she can practice her native cultural rules while in Hong Kong? Explain your answer.

GENERATE CULTURAL BEHAVIORS AND RULES

List two cultural behaviors in your contact culture that you would like more information about. Perhaps you are unsure of the appropriate cultural rules for these behaviors. Write the names of these behaviors on a slip of paper (do not write your name on the paper) and give it to your instructor.

As your teacher reads the behaviors, discuss what you think the rules are for each one.

Understanding and Using Emotions: Reading about another person's experience lets you assess your own feelings.

READING

The following passage describes a Japanese student's first homestay with an American family. She describes how her native cultural rules for gift-giving brought her security in an unfamiliar situation. As you read, compare Tsugumi's experience with Nancy's.

A JAPANESE STUDENT IN THE UNITED STATES

It was my first experience in a homestay. I wanted to take a gift for my host and hostess to show them my appreciation for their hospitality. After much thought, I decided to take a Japanese tea set to give to the family. I had learned that it was acceptable to give a gift for this occasion, but that my host and hostess would not expect me to give them a gift. I also had learned that when a gift is given for hospitality, it is usually given at the time of departure. This is different from the Japanese cultural rules for gift-giving. We like to give the host or hostess a gift upon arrival, as soon as we enter their home. However, I was determined to practice the American cultural rules and give them my teapot right before I left.

I could never have imagined how fearful and nervous I became when I entered my host family's home, and it was just me and them in a huge house. They showed me my room, and I put my luggage in the corner, and without even thinking, I took out the teapot I had brought and gave it to them. I immediately felt less nervous and more comfortable. They raved about the beauty of the teapot and set it in a special place in the living room bookcase.

I thought about my behavior that night and decided that what I had done was good. After all, I am Japanese.

–Tsugumi

Threads

"There are as many ways to look upon a thing as there are men to look upon it. That, my son, is what the truth is."

Native American Shaman in *Indian America,* by Jamake Highwater

TALK IT OVER

1. Do you agree with Tsugumi's decision to give her hostess the gift as soon as she arrived?
2. What is the difference between Tsugumi's feelings and Nancy's feelings?

JOURNAL

Cultural Rules

Have you ever had an experience like Nancy's or Tsugumi's? Describe the situation and your feelings about it. How are the rules for behaving in that situation different in your native culture and your contact culture?

CREATE AN IDEAL CULTURE

In a group with three or four classmates, design an ideal culture using the following information.

You are flying overseas on a chartered aircraft when it develops engine trouble and crash-lands on an uninhabited island. You have just enough time to grab your carry-on luggage and jump out before the plane bursts into flames. The pilot did not survive the crash. However, none of the passengers are injured. There is no chance of rescue or escape. Among the passengers, a variety of ages, nationalities, cultures, languages, and religions are represented.

With these conditions, you are left to build a life, a culture, a community for yourselves. This will obviously entail creating a structure for how you will survive and develop as a group of people. Now is your opportunity to create an ideal culture.

As you think about where and how to begin, consider these questions:

1. How will you communicate with one another?
2. How will you get food and water?
3. What will you do for living accommodations? Clothing?
4. What kind of government will you have? What laws will you make? How will you enforce those laws? What type of leadership will you have?
5. What type of work will you do? How will you make a living? Will there be different jobs for women and men? For children and adults?
6. What type of social classes will be formed?
7. What type of educational system will you establish?
8. What type of religion will you practice? What values will you uphold? What rituals or ceremonies will be a part of your worship practices?
9. What marriage, engagement, and courtship customs (or laws) will you have?
10. What will you do for entertainment? Will you have sports, recreation?

JOURNAL

Reviewing Your Journey

Review the writing activities in this chapter. What have you learned about your native culture and your contact culture? What do you understand about culture that you didn't understand before?

THE JOURNEY CONTINUES

Through the activities in this chapter, you have begun the journey to understanding your contact culture. In the chapters to come, you will learn more about the culture and the people. Along the way, you will also learn more about yourself and your native culture.

Crossing Cultures

Take part. Involve yourself. Plunge in.
Embrace new experiences.
Partake of your own life.

–John Roger and Peter McWilliams (from *Life 101*)

Wrong-Way Pedestrians Irksome Too

Since walking most certainly is a form of getting around, I pose a question: Why is it that some people refuse to stroll on the right side of the sidewalk, insisting instead on forging ahead on the left?

Do they enjoy dodging oncoming pedestrians as much as the oncomers dislike avoiding them?

Is it possible all these walkers are from England or the Bahamas or Kenya or some other country where motorists drive on the wrong side of the road?

And are these the same people who go upstream at the restaurant salad bar, bumping into the rest of us and knocking our croutons to the floor?

Gary Washburn, *Chicago Tribune,* Jan. 25, 1993

TALK IT OVER

1. Do you think the way people walk is part of culture?
2. The article describes motorists in some countries as driving on the "wrong side of the road." Why do you think the author says this?
3. What point is the author trying to make?

CONSIDER THIS

Do you enjoy living in your contact culture? Do all the behaviors you've seen in your contact culture make sense to you? Do any of the behaviors seem "wrong" to you?

_____

_____

_____

In this chapter, you will read about the experiences of people who have lived in another culture. You will also be able to think about your own experiences in your contact culture, the struggles you have had, and the adjustments you have had to make. You will discover why it is natural for people to face difficulties when they live in another culture.

Threads

"All beginnings are hard. Especially a beginning that you have to make by yourself. That's the hardest beginning of all."

Chaim Potok, *In the Beginning*

The following journal entries, written by ESL students, are descriptions of cross-cultural experiences. As you read, imagine how the writer must have felt during the experience.

READING

Culture Journals

A TIP SYSTEM

Why is there a tip system in America? We don't have a tip system in my country. So, I can't get used to it.

One time when I went to a restaurant, I gave a 15% tip with a check. But a waitress gave back change. So, I thought she didn't want a tip. So, I didn't give her a tip and I left the restaurant. She chased me outside the restaurant and said, "You didn't pay a tip! You must pay 15% tip!" I was surprised. I apologized and gave her 15% tip.

I felt ashamed of myself. But I didn't know I couldn't give a tip with a check. I guess I had a good experience because if she hadn't chased me, I still wouldn't know that. But I think that a tip should not be requested; it should be paid depending on the service.

–Ayako

TALK IT OVER

1. Why was Ayako confused? How did Ayako's native culture affect her experience with the waitress?
2. Do you think the waitress was right in chasing Ayako and asking for the tip?
3. What do you think Ayako learned about her contact culture from this experience?
4. Have you ever had a cross-cultural experience similar to Ayako's experience?

CO-ED TAE KWON DO

Last semester I took a gym class at school. It was a class in tae kwon do, a martial arts class like karate. In my class were some boys and some girls. I never had a gym class with boys and girls in the same class before. In my class, the teacher put us in pairs to practice and fight together. Sometimes the teacher put a boy and a girl together. Sometimes the boys and the girls were laughing when they practiced together. I think sometimes they fought and touched too much. If I had a daughter, I would not want her to take any gym class with boys in the class.

–Sayeed

> ### Threads
>
> **Tipping is considered to be a form of begging in Tahiti.**
>
> The Curious Book

TALK IT OVER

1. Sayeed had a new experience in school in the United States. What was new for him? Would this be a new experience for you? Would you feel the same way Sayeed did?
2. Do you think that teachers should ask male and female students to practice together in physical education? Why do you think the teacher did so here?
3. Why do you think the male and female students were laughing?
4. Did you ever experience anything new in school in your contact culture that made you feel uncomfortable? What was that experience? Did you ever experience anything new that you enjoyed a lot? What was that experience?

FAMILY BUSINESS PARTNERS

I had an opportunity to learn that Americans sometimes treat their family members as business partners.

One day my husband and I were invited to his professor's house for dinner. After dinner we chatted about families. The professor has two married daughters. One of his sons-in-law had recently fixed a fence for him and he paid the son-in-law for his work. The professor told us it had become a rule that they discussed payment before the work is to be done.

This is an interesting cultural observation for me. In a Chinese family it is considered the responsibility of young members to help the old member. The old members don't need to pay and the young members don't expect to get paid. In this way both young and old members feel the warmth of the family.

–*Ping*

TALK IT OVER

1. What did Ping learn from her experience?
2. What does Ping seem to think about this behavior?
3. Does Ping's native culture influence her interpretation? Explain.
4. Why do you think the American father-in-law paid his son-in-law for fixing the fence?
5. How would someone from your native culture interpret this practice? Do you agree with Ping's conclusion that warmth in the family is felt when younger members help the older members without being paid?

IT WORKS!
Learning Strategy:
Considering Your
Own Experience

LEARNING STRATEGY

Forming Concepts: Discussing what you read helps clarify issues.

LANGUAGE FOCUS

Inferencing

1. Look up the word *infer* in your dictionary. Write the definition in your own words in the space below.

_____

_____

_____

_____

2. Read the following statements and put a check beside the one that best represents what Ping infers.

_____ American families have more warmth than Chinese families.

_____ Chinese families have more warmth than American families.

3. What do you think Sayeed infers about American culture based on his experience?
4. Do you interpret Ping's and Sayeed's experiences in the same way they did? Do you make the same inferences?

Although Ping and Sayeed do not directly state how they feel about American culture, you can guess how they feel about it. You can *infer* how they feel based on their descriptions of their experiences.

LEARNING STRATEGY

Forming Concepts: Listening to others expands your point of view.

CONTRIBUTE YOUR IDEAS

Ayako's, Ping's, and Sayeed's experiences provide you with information to base your own inferences on.

1. What do you infer about these students' native cultures, family backgrounds, and personalities based on their journal entries?
2. Join with other classmates to discuss your answers. Did you make similar inferences?

LEARNING STRATEGY

Understanding and Using Emotions: Writing can help you become aware of your feelings.

WRITE A LETTER

Have you ever had a cross-cultural experience like Ayako's, Sayeed's or Ping's? Have you ever felt like the customs in your native culture were better than the ones in your contact culture?

Write a letter to Ping, Sayeed or Ayako and tell her or him about your experience. Describe how you felt during and after the experience.

In your letter, include at least two suggestions for adjusting to another culture.

Your awareness of your contact culture increases with the time you spend within it and with its members. However, increased awareness does not guarantee that your life in that culture will be easy. It is likely that anyone trying to adjust to a new culture will face some difficulties. The following activities will help you identify expectations you had about your contact culture before you came and the cultural struggles that you have gone through.

2.2 IDENTIFYING CULTURAL STRUGGLES

SHARE YOUR EXPERIENCE

What has been the biggest surprise for you since arriving in your contact culture? Did you have any misconceptions about what your life would be like here? If so, what were they?

READING

In the following reading, an American woman living in the former Soviet Union explains her earlier misconceptions and later surprises about life there.

THE BIGGEST SURPRISES

During my first visit to the Soviet Union in 1988, I thought I was visiting a great superpower, but I found myself in a Third World country. We once heard it described as "upper Volta with rockets." Now I'm surprised that things that frustrated me a year ago don't bother me so much now. I still don't like the general state of disrepair and the inefficiency, but I'm getting used to them. If I go to take a shower and there's no hot water, it's not a crisis. If I make an appointment and the person doesn't show, I figure they're waiting for a bus somewhere or simply running on "Russian time," and I don't take it personally.

–*Cheryl*

VOCABULARY FOCUS

Phrases

With a classmate, discuss the following questions about phrases from the passage above.

1. What does "Third World country" mean?
2. Why was the Soviet Union described as "Upper Volta with rockets"?
3. What does Cheryl mean when she says, "It's not a crisis"?
4. What is "Russian time"?

TALK IT OVER

1. What were Cheryl's expectations of the Soviet Union before she moved there?
2. Cheryl claims she is surprised that things that frustrated her a year ago don't bother her so much now. What examples does she give of adjustments she has made?

LEARNING STRATEGY

Forming Concepts: Comparing and contrasting cultures provide a basis for understanding.

WRITE ABOUT IT

If you are a female, write about the first question below. If you are a male, write about the second question.

A. What are the struggles of women who come from your native culture to live in your contact culture? What is difficult for them? What kinds of adjustments do they have to make?

B. What are the struggles of men who come from your native culture to live in your contact culture? What is difficult for them? What kinds of adjustments do they have to make?

CONSIDER THIS

The following essay was written by an American woman who lives in Odessa. She describes several cultural struggles that foreign women face in Odessa. What struggles might face a member of your contact culture who lives in your native culture?

READING

As you read this essay, focus on the cultural struggles the author identifies and be prepared to discuss them.

CULTURAL STRUGGLES

On a physical level, women here (both nationals and the rest of us) are just plain tired. The work load is immense, and simple tasks take much longer to complete than they would in the United States. If I can get three meals on the table and have a clean kitchen by 10 p.m., I've had a successful day. It takes time to peel potatoes and carrots, cut up and grind meat for hamburger, clean chickens, boil milk and water, and hunt for new recipes using cabbage.

In addition to dealing with fatigue, living here is like taking a ride on an emotional roller coaster. Small victories and insignificant disappointments alike set off major fireworks, for good or bad. A routine trip to the market can leave one feeling exhilarated ("I found decent laundry detergent today!") or depressed ("I wouldn't mind having less mud, more courtesy, and meat that hasn't been handled by the general public"). When it takes so much energy just to live and maintain a household, there's not much left for inspiring family relationships and friendships.

Then add the handicap of being a novice in the language (and when does one find time to study anyway?). None of us has lived here long, and most are new to Russian. A limited ability to communicate limits everything—the depth of relationships with nationals, the ability to get simple things done, and the amount of independence we can cling to. Many Americans go nuts over having to depend on other people for help because people tend to be incredibly unreliable. Nationals don't like to say no, so they are quick to make promises they can't keep. (Even after hearing "I'll be there tomorrow" several times, we waited four months for a friend to improve our washing machine hook-up before we finally got wise and hired another guy to do it for dollars. He came right away.) Americans like to get things done quickly, know what they can count on, and be in charge of their own affairs. It's a real cultural clash, undoubtedly frustrating on both sides.

Another cultural tension is between Russian communal thinking and American independence. Russians not only feel it is their right to tell you what to do (or what you're doing wrong)—it is their responsibility. We don't like people telling us our children aren't dressed warmly enough or shouldn't suck their thumbs or shouldn't drink cold water. When my three-year-old is having a temper tantrum outside the bread store, I'd rather not have a herd of old ladies interfering. Even though I know they feel obligated because they think they're everybody's grandma, it's still sometimes hard to blow it off.

–*Cheryl Warner*

LEARNING STRATEGY

Remembering New Material: Discussing the meaning of new idioms reinforces your memory.

VOCABULARY FOCUS

Idioms

1. Several phrases in the reading are idioms. The meanings of idioms usually cannot be found in a dictionary nor can they be interpreted literally. Read the essay again and underline the phrases you think are idioms.
2. With a partner, choose three of the idioms you underlined and discuss the possible meanings each could have.
3. With your classmates, decide which of these possible meanings best fit the context of the essay.

TALK IT OVER

1. How does the author of the essay describe Americans? Russians?
2. The author describes the physical, emotional, and cultural difficulties of adjusting to a new culture. Find two specific examples she identifies of each difficulty.
3. The author's views of Russian culture have been influenced by her experience. What makes someone react in a particular way to another culture? Does everyone react in the same way?

2.3 PERSONALIZING CULTURAL ADJUSTMENT

RECORD YOUR FEELINGS

Living in a new culture means making adjustments. What are the three hardest adjustments you have had to make while living in your contact culture? These adjustments may include adapting to different food, styles of dress, or to the things people own. You might also think about behaviors such as the way people manage time, the kinds of relationships people have, or the way parents treat their children.

In the following chart, record your adjustments, your feelings about the adjustments, and your reasons for feeling that way. Try to be specific.

WHAT I HAVE HAD TO ADJUST TO	HOW I FEEL ABOUT THIS ADJUSTMENT	WHY I FEEL THIS WAY

SHARE YOUR EXPERIENCE

1. Choose one adjustment from your chart to share with your classmates.
2. Why do you think people adjusting to the same culture may have different things to get used to?
3. Do you think adjustment is more difficult for people from certain cultural backgrounds? Explain.

2.4 REFLECTING ON WHAT YOU HAVE LEARNED 1

WRITE ABOUT IT

If you could travel back to the time before you came to your contact culture, knowing all that you know now, what would you do differently? How would you prepare? What would you bring with you or leave behind?

Write a letter to someone from your native culture who is planning to move to your contact culture. Describe some of the cultural struggles you have experienced and give advice about how to prepare for these cultural struggles.

JOURNAL

Reviewing Your Journey
What is the process of adjustment that you have gone through? How are you different now from the way you were when you first came to your contact culture? What changes have you made, and how have you made those changes?

THE JOURNEY CONTINUES

Through the activities in this chapter you have studied various cross-cultural experiences and the cultural struggles that are a natural part of living in a different culture. Chapter 3 takes you deeper into the study of culture by discussing how worldview—the way a person thinks about and sees the world—is related to cultural behavior.

Understanding Worldview

If your eyes are sound, your whole body will be full of light.

–St. Luke

The following excerpt is taken from the novel *Till We Have Faces,* by C. S. Lewis—a retelling of the Greek legend of Cupid and Psyche. In Lewis's version of the myth, Orual, the eldest daughter of Trom, King of Glome, is not beautiful. In the following passage, Orual describes how wearing a veil that covers her face makes her mysterious to the curious people in her kingdom.

. . . My second strength lay in my veil. I could never have believed, till I had proof of it, what it would do for me. From the very first, . . . as soon as my face was invisible, people began to discover all manner of beauties in my voice. At first it was "deep as a man's, but nothing in the world less mannish;" later, and

until it grew cracked with age, it was the voice of a spirit. . . . And as years passed and there were fewer in the city . . . who remembered my face, the wildest stories got about as to what that veil hid. No one believed it was anything so common as the face of an ugly woman. Some said (nearly all the younger women said) that it was frightful beyond endurance; a pig's, bear's, cat's or elephant's face. The best story was that I had no face at all; if you stripped off my veil you'd find emptiness. But another sort (there were more of the men among these) said that I wore a veil because I was of a beauty so dazzling that if I let it be seen all men in the world would run mad; or else that Ungit was jealous of my beauty and had promised to blast me if I went bareface. The upshot of all this nonsense was that I became something very mysterious and awful. . . .

–C. S. Lewis, *Till We Have Faces*

TALK IT OVER

1. How do you think Orual felt before she began wearing the veil? How did she feel after she began wearing the veil?
2. How do the opinions of other people affect the way we see ourselves?

3. Everyone has an identity. How do you feel your identity in your native culture compares to your identity in your contact culture? Do people in your contact culture see you in the same way people from home see you?

4. How is one's identity shaped by culture or language? Do you think a person's identity changes when he or she is in a contact culture or speaks a language different from his or her native language?

CONSIDER THIS

Do you ever feel that you wear a different face—a "veil"—in your contact culture than you do in your native culture? How do you think others view you? How do you view yourself?

_____

_____

_____

In this chapter you will learn about worldview. Worldview includes how you see yourself and how you see the world. The activities in this chapter will help you understand how cross-cultural misunderstandings are often a result of different worldviews.

3.1 DIFFERENT PERSPECTIVES

TALK IT OVER

Look carefully at the picture below.

1. What do you see? Do all your classmates agree on what they see in the picture?

2. How is it possible for individuals to look at the same picture and have different interpretations?

LEARNING STRATEGY

Forming Concepts: Analogies make abstract concepts more understandable.

READING

What Is Worldview?

As the picture illustrates, much of how a person sees something or understands something comes from the way in which they are looking at it. You have heard the story of the blind men who went to "see" an elephant. One of the men felt the elephant's tail. "The elephant is like a snake!" he said. Another blind man felt one of the elephant's legs. "Oh, no!" he said, "The elephant is like a tree." A third blind man felt the ear of the elephant. "Both of you are wrong," he announced. "The elephant is just like a fan."

Clearly, each man was speaking from his own experience; that the first blind man compared the elephant's tail to a snake reveals his experience with snakes. When studying culture, a similar situation exists. Every person has a particular way of seeing or interpreting the world and a particular perspective on how he or she fits in that world. This perspective comes from his or her experiences and is called **worldview.**

Our worldview influences the way we interpret reality and the way we behave. It is like a pair of glasses. Each individual wears the worldview glasses from his or her culture.

MEXICAN

AFRICAN

RUSSIAN

JAPANESE

When you wear Chinese glasses in a Korean culture, you see the culture through a Chinese perspective. You are, therefore, unable to understand the Korean culture the way Koreans do. To increase your understanding of your contact culture, you need to learn how the people interpret behavior. You need to see their world from their perspective; you need to understand their worldview. Understanding the worldview of another culture requires you to learn about the cultural behaviors, the rules for the behaviors, and the values associated with the behaviors.

TALK IT OVER

1. Where do you think a person's worldview originates?
2. Do you think all members of a culture share exactly the same worldview? Explain your answer.
3. What factors contribute to worldview? How does a person's individual background or education shape his or her worldview?

CHECKPOINT

Regardless of how worldview is conceived or whether or not the members of each culture share an identical worldview, the point is that people have different interpretations of experience, and many times these interpretations are related to their cultural backgrounds. Because of this, not only do we see things differently, but we also sometimes see things that do not exist.

CONNECT THE DOTS

Without raising your pencil off the page, connect all nine dots using four straight lines.

```
•   •   •

•   •   •

•   •   •
```

CONTRIBUTE YOUR IDEAS

Share your answer to the previous activity with your class. Did you all get the same results?

If connecting all nine dots with four consecutive straight lines was difficult for you, perhaps it was because you saw a "square" when you looked at the dots. Although the dots are arranged in a square, the square does not exist; it is in your imagination.

Everyone interprets experience based on the knowledge he or she has already. Sometimes this knowledge is helpful; other times it can hinder understanding. The following activities illustrate what can happen when two worldviews collide.

Threads

"The only way to make a man trustworthy is to trust him."

Henry L. Stimson

WRITE ABOUT IT

Before you read the following story, write about a time in which you were confused because you did not understand what you were seeing or experiencing. Describe the experience and how you finally discovered what was happening.

CONTRIBUTE YOUR IDEAS

1. The title of the following story is "You Have Left Your Lotus Pods on the Bus." There are five main characters in the story: two American men and three Thai monks. The American men and the Thai monks spend a day together exploring Thailand. What do you know about Thailand? What do you know about Thai monks? What do you know about American men?

2. Based on the information in the title and what you believe about the characters in the story, what do you predict the story to be about?

3. Read the first paragraph of the story. Then answer these questions: How would you describe the American's first impression of the monks and the monks' first impressions of the American? What ideas do you now have about the story?

4. The second paragraph introduces the rest of the characters in the story. Read this paragraph and write three ideas you have about the story. What do you think will happen?

   a. _____

   b. _____

   c. _____

READING

YOU HAVE LEFT YOUR LOTUS PODS ON THE BUS
Adapted from the story by Paul Bowles

Part I: First Encounter
. . . Brooks, teaching at Chulalongkorn University, was required as a Fulbright Fellow to attend regular classes in Thai; as an **adjunct** to this he arranged to spend much of his leisure time with Thais. One day he brought along with him three young men wearing the bright orange-yellow robes of Buddhist monks. They filed into the hotel room in silence and stood in a row as they were presented to me, each one responding by joining his palms together, thumbs touching his chest.

As we talked, Yamyong, the eldest, in his late twenties, explained that he was an **ordained** monk, while the other two were **novices**. . . . He glanced up at me and went on talking. "Your room is beautiful. We are not accustomed to such luxury." His voice was flat; he was trying to conceal his disapproval. The three **conferred** briefly in undertones. "My friends say they have never seen such a luxurious room," he reported, watching me closely through his steel-rimmed spectacles to see my reaction. I failed to hear. . . .

Time went on, and we sat there, extending but not altering the subject of conversation. Occasionally I looked around the room. Before they had come in, it had been only a hotel room whose curtains must be kept drawn. Their presence and their comments on it had managed to **invest** it with a vaguely disturbing quality; I felt that they considered it a great mistake on my part to have chosen such a place in which to stay.

"Look at his tattoo," said Brooks. "Show him."

Yamyong pulled back his robe a bit from the shoulder, and I saw the two indigo lines of finely written Thai characters. "That is for good health," he said, glancing up at me. His smile seemed odd, but then, his facial expression did not complement his words at any point.

"Don't the Buddhists disapprove of tattooing?" I said.

"Some people say it is backwardness." Again he smiled. "Words for good health are said to be **superstition.** This was done by my **abbot** when I was a boy studying in the wat. Perhaps he did not know it was a superstition."

We were about to go with them to visit the wat where they lived. I pulled a tie from the closet and stood before the mirror arranging it.

"Sir," Yamyong began. "Will you please explain something? What is the significance of the necktie?"

"The significance of the necktie?" I turned to face him. "You mean, why do men wear neckties?"

"No. I know that. The purpose is to look like a gentleman."

I laughed. Yamyong was not put off. "I have noticed that some men wear the two ends equal, and some wear the wide end longer than the narrow, or the narrow longer than the wide. And the neckties themselves, they are not all the same length, are they? Some even with both ends equal reach below the waist. What are the different meanings?"

"There is no meaning," I said. "Absolutely none.". . .

"I believe you, of course," he said graciously. "But we all thought each way had a different significance attached."

As we went out of the hotel, the doorman bowed respectfully. Until now he had never given a sign that he was aware of my existence. The wearers of the yellow robe **carry weight** in Thailand.

Vocabulary

adjunct: addition
ordained: appointed, given the total responsibilities of a monk
novices: people in training to become religious leaders
conferred: had a conversation
invest: give
superstition: trust in magic or chance
abbot: the leader in a religious house for men
carry weight: are important

LEARNING STRATEGY

Managing Your Learning: Dividing a reading into parts helps you understand the meaning of the whole.

CONTRIBUTE YOUR IDEAS

In Part I of the story, there are three main topics of discussion:

1. The luxurious hotel room
2. Yamyong's tattoo
3. The significance of the necktie

Read Part I of the story again. What cultural differences are shown in the conversations about these topics? Write one or two sentences explaining the misunderstandings.

_____

_____

_____

_____

_____

_____

_____

READING

YOU HAVE LEFT YOUR LOTUS PODS ON THE BUS

Part II: A Sunday Excursion

A few Sundays later I agreed to go with Brooks and our friends to Ayudhaya. . . . We got to a bus terminal on the northern outskirts of the city.

It was a nice, old-fashioned, open bus. . . . Brooks, in high spirits, kept calling across to me: "Look! Water buffaloes!" As we went further away from Bangkok there were more of the beasts, and his cries became more frequent. Yamyong, sitting next to me, whispered: "Professor Brooks is fond of buffaloes?" I laughed and said I didn't think so.

"Then?"

I said that in America there were no buffaloes in the fields, and that was why Brooks was interested in seeing them. There were no temples in the landscape, either, I told him and added, perhaps unwisely: "He looks at buffaloes. I look at

temples." This struck Yamyong as **hilarious,** and he made **allusions** to it now and then all during the day. . . .

At the first stop the **bhikkus** got out. They came aboard again with mangosteens and lotus pods and insisted on giving us large numbers of each. . . . "Something new for you today, I think," Yamyong said with a satisfied air. . . .

The bus's last stop was still two or three miles from the center of Ayudhaya. We got down into the dust, and Brooks declared: "The first thing we must do is find food. They can't eat anything solid, you know, after midday."

"Not noon exactly," Yamyong said. "Maybe one o'clock or a little later."
"Even so, that doesn't leave much time," I told him. "It's quarter to twelve now."

But the bhikkus were not hungry. None of them had visited Ayudhaya before, and so they had **compiled** a list of things they most wanted to see. . . .

When we got back to the bus stop, the subject of food arose once again, but the **excursion** had put the bhikkus into such a state of excitement that they could not bear to **allot** time for anything but looking. We went to the museum. It was quiet; there were Khmer heads and documents inscribed in Pali. The day had begun to be painful. I told myself I had known beforehand that it would. . . . I thought: If only I could get something to eat, I wouldn't mind the heat so much.

We got into the center of Ayudhaya a little after three o'clock. It was hot and noisy; the bhikkus had no idea of where to look for a restaurant, and the prospect of asking did not appeal to them. The five of us walked **aimlessly.** I had come to the conclusion that neither Prasert nor Vichai understood spoken English, and I addressed myself earnestly to Yamyong. "We've got to eat." He stared at me with severity. "We are searching," he told me.

Eventually we found a Chinese restaurant on a corner of the principal street. . . .

The large menu in English which was brought us must have been typed several decades ago and wiped with a damp rag once a week ever since. Under the heading SPECIALTIES were some dishes that caught my eye, and as I went through the list I began to laugh. Then I read it aloud to Brooks.

"FRIED SHARKS FINS AND BEAN SPROUT
CHICKEN CHINS STUFFED WITH SHRIMP
FRIED RICE BIRDS
SHRIMPS BALLS AND GREEN MARROW
PIGS LIGHTS WITH PICKLES
BRAKED RICE BIRD IN PORT WINE
FISH HEAD AND BEAN CURD"

Although it was natural for our friends not to join in the laughter, I felt that their silence was not merely failure to respond; it was heavy, **positive.**

A moment later three Pepsi-Cola bottles were brought and placed on the table. "What are you going to have?" Brooks asked Yamyong.

"Nothing, thank you," he said lightly. "This will be enough for us today."

"But this is terrible! You mean no one is going to eat anything?"

"You and your friend will eat your food," said Yamyong. (He might as well have said **"fodder."**) Then he, Prasert, and Vichai stood up, and carrying their Pepsi-Cola bottles with them, went to sit at a table on the other side of the room. Now and then Yamyong smiled sternly across at us.

"I wish they'd stop watching us," Brooks said under his breath.

"They were the ones who kept putting it off," I reminded him. But I felt guilty, and I was annoyed at finding myself placed in the position of the **self-indulgent** unbeliever. It was almost as bad as eating in front of Moslems during Ramadan.

We finished our meal and set out immediately, following Yamyong's decision to visit a certain temple he wanted to see. . . .

Brooks sat beside me on the bus going back to Bangkok. We spoke only now and then. After so many hours of resisting the heat, it was relaxing to sit and feel the relatively cool air that blew in from the rice fields. . . . I might even have dozed off, had there not been in the back of the bus a man, obviously not in control, who was intent on making as much noise as possible. He began to shout, scream, and howl almost as soon as we had left Ayudhaya, and he did this consistently throughout the journey. Brooks and I laughed about it, **conjecturing** whether he was crazy or only drunk. . . . Occasionally I glanced at the other passengers. It was as though they were entirely unaware of the **commotion** behind them. As we drew closer to the city, the screams became louder and almost constant.

"God, why don't they throw him off?" Brooks was beginning to be annoyed.

"They don't even hear him," I said bitterly. People who can **tolerate** noise inspire me with envy and rage. Finally I leaned over and said to Yamyong: "That poor man back there! It's incredible!"

"Yes," he said over his shoulder. "He's very busy." This set me thinking what a civilized and tolerant people they were, and I **marvelled** at the sophistication of the word "busy" to describe what was going on in the back of the bus.

Finally we were in a taxi driving across Bangkok. . . . In my head I was still hearing the heartrending cries. What had the repeated word patterns meant?

I had not been able to give an acceptable answer to Yamyong in his **bewilderment** about the significance of the necktie, but perhaps he could satisfy my curiosity here.

"That man in the back of the bus, you know?"

Yamyong nodded. "He was working very hard, poor fellow. Sunday is a bad day."

I disregarded the nonsense. "What was he saying?"

"Oh, he was saying: 'Go into second gear,' or 'We are coming to a bridge,' or 'Be careful, people in the road.' What he saw."

Since neither Brooks nor I appeared to have understood, he went on. "All the buses must have a driver's assistant. He watches that road and tells the driver how to drive. It is hard work because he must shout loud enough for the driver to hear him."

"But why doesn't he sit up in front with the driver?"

"No, no. There must be one in front and one in the back. That way two men are responsible for the bus."

It was an unconvincing explanation for the **grueling** sounds we had heard, but to show him that I believed him I said: "Aha! I see."

The taxi drew up in front of the hotel and I got out. When I said good-by to Yamyong, he replied, I think with a shade of **aggrievement:** "Good-bye. You have left your lotus pods on the bus."

Vocabulary

hilarious: very funny

allusions: references

bhikkus: monks

compiled: put together

excursion: trip

allot: give, set aside

aimlessly: without a purpose or goal

positive: full of meaning

fodder: food for animals

self-indulgent: selfish, concerned mainly with one's own needs

conjecturing: discussing, guessing

commotion: noise, disorder

tolerate: put up with, be patient with

marvelled: was amazed, surprised by

bewilderment: confusion

grueling: terrible

aggrievement: offense, feeling wronged

CONTRIBUTE YOUR IDEAS

In Part II, three situations arise that reflect cultural differences:

1. Brook's interest in the buffaloes
2. The issues of lunch
3. The driver's assistant

What differences between American and Thai monk culture does each situation reveal? Write a few sentences explaining the differences.

Threads

"Speak the truth but leave immediately after."

Slovenian Proverb

LEARNING STRATEGY

Understanding and Using Emotions: Talking about your emotional reaction right away lets you analyze other things later with less bias.

TALK IT OVER

1. What in the story did you enjoy the most? Was there anything about this story you did not like?
2. What do you infer was the monks' impression of the Americans?
3. What do you infer was the Americans' impression of the monks?
4. Why was it difficult for the American men and the Thai monks to understand each other?
5. The Thai monks and the American men sometimes laughed at different things. For example, the monks laughed at the Americans for being excited about seeing buffaloes and temples; the Americans laughed at the restaurant menus. Why do you think people from different cultures laugh at different things?

LEARNING STRATEGY

Forming Concepts: Discussing your views with others stimulates ideas.

CONTRIBUTE YOUR IDEAS

Cultural misunderstandings may occur because people have different customs, behaviors, or practices, each of which is influenced by worldview. Knowing what people value, or view as important, helps you understand their worldview.

1. Review your descriptions of the cultural differences that arose in the first part of the story. Each difference represents a clash in worldview. For example, Yamyong's comment about the luxurious hotel room makes better sense when we understand that monks place a high value on living without material possessions or luxury. Material possessions are viewed as unnecessary, or even "sinful."

   List the two other topics of conversation in Part I. Identify the competing values or beliefs of the Americans and the Thais.
2. Review the part of the story that describes the experience at the Chinese restaurant. Why wouldn't the monks eat anything? Why did Brooks and his friend feel like "self-indulgent unbelievers"? What clashes in *cultural values* can you identify?
3. Recall the second part of the story. How did the Americans view the man in the back of the bus? How did their understanding change when Yamyong informed them that the man was the driver's assistant?
4. The last line in the story reads: "Good-bye. You have left your lotus pods on the bus." How do you think the monks felt about the Americans forgetting their lotus pods on the bus?
5. The last line of the story is also the title of the story. To understand the meaning of this line and the title, you must know the *cultural value* that Thai people place on lotus pods. Why did the monks give the Americans lotus pods? What value do you think this action represents? What value do you think lotus pods have for Thais?
6. What do you think the Americans learned about Thai culture and worldview? What do you think the Thais learned about Americans?

Threads

During a Hindu wedding ceremony, a gold ornament on a knotted yellow string is tied around the bride's neck to remind her of her duty to her parents, husband, and sons.

Bride's Magazine

CONSIDER THIS

What does it mean to "think like a Thai," or "think like a German," or "think like an Mexican," or "think like an American"? If people from the same culture share a common worldview, what does that mean? How can that be described?

READING

The following reading is from an article by Amy Tan, a Chinese-American linguist and fiction writer. The passage describes an interaction between Amy and her aunt and uncle who have come from Beijing to visit her in the United States. The aunt and uncle had been in the United States for three months, and on their last night, Amy wanted to take them out to dinner.

"YOU THINK CHINESE"

"Are you hungry?" I asked in Chinese.

"Not hungry," said my uncle promptly, the same response he once gave me ten minutes before he suffered a low-blood-sugar attack.

"Not too hungry," said my aunt. "Perhaps you're hungry?"

"A little," I admitted.

"We can eat, we can eat," they both consented.

"What kind of food?" I asked.

"Oh, doesn't matter. Anything will do. Nothing fancy, just some simple food is fine."

"Do you like Japanese food? We haven't had that yet," I suggested.

They looked at each other.

"We can eat it," said my uncle bravely, this survivor of the Long March.

"We have eaten it before," added my aunt. "Raw fish."

"Oh, you don't like it?" I said. "Don't be polite. We can go somewhere else."

"We are not being polite. We can eat it," my aunt insisted.

So I drove them to Japantown and we walked past several restaurants featuring colorful plastic displays of sushi.

"Not this one, not this one either," I continued to say, as if searching for a Japanese restaurant similar to the last. "Here it is," I finally said, turning into a restaurant famous for its Chinese fish dishes from Shandong.

"Oh, Chinese food!" cried my aunt, obviously relieved.

My uncle patted my arm. "You think Chinese."

"It's your last night here in America," I said. "So don't be polite. Act like an American."

And that night we ate a banquet.

Overcoming Limitations: Analyzing real situations helps make abstract concepts more concrete.

TALK IT OVER

1. How were the aunt and uncle being "polite"?
2. What kind of restaurant was Amy searching for? How did the aunt and uncle feel when they saw that the Japanese restaurant served Chinese food?
3. Why did Amy's uncle pat her arm and say, "You think Chinese"?
4. What did Amy mean when she said, "So don't be polite. Act like an American."
5. How might an American have handled the dinner arrangement?

Testing Hypotheses: Using dialogues promotes your understanding of new concepts.

CREATE A DIALOGUE

Using the theme of the Amy Tan passage above, create a dialogue between a native of your contact culture and the Chinese aunt and uncle. What would happen if Amy's character were played by someone from your contact culture?

CONTRIBUTE YOUR IDEAS

Share your dialogue with your classmates. Discuss how each dialogue represents an understanding of the worldview of your contact culture. Do you agree or disagree with your classmates' conclusions about your contact culture?

3.4 REFLECTING ON WHAT YOU HAVE LEARNED

SHARE YOUR EXPERIENCE

Talk about a cross-cultural misunderstanding you have had in your contact culture that demonstrates a clash in worldviews. What specific cultural differences caused the misunderstanding? Was there a conflict in values as well? What did you learn from this misunderstanding?

LEARNING STRATEGY

Forming Concepts: Writing a summary allows you to organize information.

JOURNAL

Reviewing Your Journey

What did you learn from this chapter about the concept of worldview? Write a summary of your discoveries.

THE JOURNEY CONTINUES

In the first three chapters of this book, you have been introduced to various aspects of culture, studied other people's cross-cultural experiences and seen that worldview is often the root of cross-cultural misunderstandings. But how can you further discover the worldview of people in your contact culture? How can you understand the way they think or interpret experience?

Chapter 4 introduces you to a technique for increasing your knowledge of your contact culture. This technique, called guided observation, is used by anthropologists while studying different cultures. When using this technique, you will be able to observe more closely and accurately the behaviors of people in your contact culture. And through observing what people do, you will come to understand their worldview and the values that they hold.

Observing Culture

"Well," said Owl, "the customary procedure in such cases is as follows."

"What does Crustimoney Proseedcake mean?" said Pooh. "For I am a Bear of Very Little Brain, and long words Bother me."

"It means the Things to Do."

"As long as it means that, I don't mind," said Pooh humbly.

–A.A. Milne

CHAPTER 4

Bus journeys were a more difficult adventure. "The caseworker told us the numbers of the bus we were supposed to take to the office. He says to take number 20 downtown, then get off and wait for number 9 that will take you to the office. When you go back, you take number 9 back downtown, then get on 20 to go back home. But there were many things he didn't mention,

like for instance that you have to pay. It must have looked funny—bus stops, doors open, a group of Asians gets on bus, doors close, doors open, Asians get off bus. Then when we know we have to pay, we get on with dollar bills and bus driver won't take them. Must have change. We can't understand driver, driver can't understand us. Just thinks we are dumb. Then you figure out that you have to get change and get it and get back on bus, but don't know how much you are supposed to put in so you ask driver and he doesn't understand. Pretty soon, he just wants you off the bus! So we watch. We watch people drop the coins in and we count and learn how much to drop in. Then we ride the bus. But we don't know how to get off, how to make the bus stop. So we ride and ride the bus until the driver looks at us like he thinks there's something wrong with us, so we get off. And we get on another bus and get lost. Then we walk.". . .

"Because I am a good Cambodian boy, I keep my head down, my eyes down, so I never see Americans pull the cord to ring the bell to signal to driver to stop. I hear the bell, and I notice that the bus stops, but by the time I look up at the sound of the bell, the cord has been pulled and I don't see how to do it. Then, one day, I am on the bus, about to be lost again, when I see an old, old lady. She is ahead of me and I see her raise her arm, very slow, very shaky, and I wonder what she is doing. I keep watching as her arm goes up, slowly, slowly, reaches something by the window, and pulls and I hear the bell, and aha! I know how to make the bell ring! So I don't get lost this time. And I go home and teach everybody. I gather everybody and tell them how you have to pull down on cord to make the bell ring and I am so happy that I can help everyone, teach them how not to get lost. That old lady was a good teacher to me."

–Paul Thai, *Imagining America*

TALK IT OVER

1. Why does Paul say the old lady "was a good teacher"? How did she "teach" Paul how to stop the bus?
2. Sometimes, when language does not prove the best way to gather information, we have to call upon other tools. What skill did Paul use to increase his knowledge of bus-riding behavior?
3. Have you had an experience similar to Paul's? Have you learned how to do something by watching others?

CONSIDER THIS

How do you think observation can help you learn about your contact culture? What role does observation have in helping you to learn something new?

_____

_____

_____

_____

_____

_____

_____

_____

Through the activities in Chapters 1, 2, and 3, you began your journey to cultural understanding by increasing your cultural awareness and considering the process of cultural adjustment. You completed these activities by calling upon your experiences in both your native and contact cultures. While experience is a useful source of information, observation is a more objective way to acquire cultural understanding. In this chapter, you will learn techniques for observing cultural behavior. You will apply these techniques throughout the remainder of this text.

4.1 INTRODUCING OBSERVATION

READING

CULTURAL BEHAVIOR AND OBSERVATION

Human behavior is not unplanned. Rather, it is the product of the knowledge and observance of a set of rules. Every culture has its own rules that guide what its members do and how they think. What someone does and how he/she thinks when influenced by his/her culture is a cultural behavior.

Our key task in understanding a culture is observing the members of the culture as they behave. Ideally, as we observe the behaviors, we learn how to participate in the behaviors. However, cultural membership involves more than being able to demonstrate particular behaviors. Aside from sharing behaviors and rules for these behaviors, the members of a culture share knowledge of why these behaviors are important for the culture. Uncovering this knowledge is not easy. The reasons for and meaning of a behavior cannot be observed. They may be assumed or inferred from the data we have collected through observation. And they may be verified by asking members of the culture their views on the reasons and meanings.

WHAT DO YOU SEE?

Task One

Your teacher will give you one minute to look at the picture below. When that minute is over, you will close your books, join with a classmate, and together note down everything you remember seeing in the picture.

Task Two

Cover the picture and answer the following questions without looking at the picture, and relying on only your memory and your notes.

1. What are the people doing?
2. How many newspaper vending machines are there?
3. What is the man carrying?
4. Are any of the women wearing hats?
5. What type of transportation is in the picture?

Task Three

Now, with the picture in front of you, answer the questions again.

TALK IT OVER

1. Compare the observations you made in Tasks 1, 2, and 3. In Task 1, your observations were based solely on your memory. In Task 2, your observations were still based on your memory but were triggered by questions. In Task 3, you were able to use the questions as you observed the picture. Which task was easier? Why?
2. Review the observations you made in Tasks 1, 2, and 3. What effect did the questions have on your observations?

4.2 THE INGREDIENTS OF BEHAVIOR

You have learned the importance of questions in helping you focus your observations. The observations you will be making as you try to increase your understanding of your contact culture will focus on cultural behaviors. All cultural behaviors, whatever their function, are organized similarly. The following questions identify the ingredients of cultural behaviors. These ingredients are either observable or inferable in all of the cultural behaviors you will be observing and analyzing.

LEARNING STRATEGY

Managing Your Learning: Using questions can structure your observations.

OBSERVATION QUESTIONS

Individuals:	Whom do you see?
Background:	Where are they? What objects and materials are also present?
Activities:	What are they doing?
Expressions:	What are they saying?
Order:	What happened before this behavior began? What will happen next? How long have they been there? How long will they remain?
Rules:	What must individuals do to participate appropriately in this behavior?
Hopes:	What is the purpose of the behavior? What do the individuals want to accomplish?
Values:	Why is this behavior important? What does it reveal about the individuals and their culture?

OBSERVATION TASK

Describing a Picture

Look at the picture below and listen to the audio tape as your teacher plays it. Write a detailed description of what you saw and heard as you answer the Observation Questions.

IDENTIFYING BEHAVIOR

In answering the previous questions, you have described and defined a behavior. Name the behavior occurring in the photograph.

CONTRIBUTE YOUR IDEAS

How do your description of the photograph and your responses to the questions compare with a classmate's?

1. Did you respond to the questions in the same way?
2. Did you assign the same name to the behavior?
3. Which questions could you answer purely from information in the picture?
4. Which questions did you need more information to answer? How did you find this information?

CHECKPOINT

As you attempt to understand culture, you will be observing innumerable situations and behaviors. Whatever cultural behaviors you observe, you will be able to answer the same set of eight questions about those behaviors. Every behavior is composed of the same set of eight ingredients. Some of these ingredients are observable. Others require you to make inferences.

The *BEHAVIOR* Acronym

You have been introduced to the ingredients of cultural behavior in the Observation Questions on page 45 To help you remember them, write the appropriate ingredient next to each letter below. When you finish, look at the first letter of each ingredient. The acronym spells **BEHAVIOR.**

B _____

E _____

H _____

A _____

V _____

I _____

O _____

R _____

NOTE: The BEHAVIOR model and the Observation Questions are reprinted in Appendix A so you may refer to them as you undertake observation tasks throughout this text.

4.3 PRACTICING OBSERVATION WITH THE BEHAVIOR MODEL

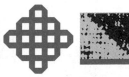

LEARNING STRATEGY

Managing Your Learning: Taking notes helps you organize your ideas.

OBSERVATION TASK

Photographs of Your Contact Culture
1. Find photographs in newspapers or magazines or in your own collection that show people involved in behaviors common in your contact culture. Bring these photographs to class.
2. In class, look at the photographs.
3. With a few of your classmates, choose a photograph you are all interested in analyzing for information about your contact culture.
4. Apply the BEHAVIOR model and respond to the Observation Questions. Be sure to write down your analysis.

OBSERVATION TASK

Photographs of Another Culture

1. Explore your personal collection of photographs of your native culture. Find one or more photographs of people involved in behaviors common in your native culture.
2. Exchange photographs with a classmate. Using the BEHAVIOR model, analyze the cultural behavior in the photograph.
3. When you have completed your analysis of your classmate's photograph, return the photo and discuss your findings and interpretation. According to your classmate, how accurate was your analysis?

Threads

A water fountain in a front yard in Morocco symbolizes wealth because water there is very scarce.

The Curious Book,

TALK IT OVER

Photographs are one source of information you can observe to learn about cultural behavior. Yet photographs are limited because they are static.

1. What information about cultural behavior is difficult to observe in a photograph?
2. Which ingredients are more difficult to identify in a photograph than they would be in live behavior?

4.4 REFINING YOUR OBSERVATION SKILLS

A better source of cultural data is on-going behavior that you, yourself, have participated in. The next set of tasks requires you to focus on a behavior that takes place within your contact culture and that you are already very familiar with.

OBSERVATION TASK

Describing Teaching and Learning in Your Classroom

Think of a typical day in your class. As you consider the following questions, make some brief notes.

1. Who is present in your classroom?
2. What activities do they participate in?
3. In what order do these activities occur?
4. What do the individuals in your classroom say?
5. What are the goals of the individuals in your classroom? Why are they there?
6. How is the classroom set up? What materials do the participants use when they are learning?
7. What do you and your classmates think is important? What values do you share while you are in class? (For example, respect for the teacher)
8. What rules do individuals need to follow in your class? How do you know where to sit, when to talk, and when to leave?

TALK IT OVER

List on the blackboard all the rules of teaching and learning behavior in your classroom. Which rules do most of your classmates agree exist and which do they not agree about?

CONSIDER THIS

Looking back on behavior you have participated in is another useful source of cultural information. It is not as valuable, however, as behavior you both participate in and observe as it happens. Why do you think observation and analysis of behavior as it occurs is a more valuable path to cultural understanding than analysis of behavior after it has occurred?

_____

_____

_____

4.5 CONDUCTING NATURAL OBSERVATION

Through your descriptions and analyses of both the photographs and your own classroom, you have practiced using the BEHAVIOR model as a technique for increasing your cultural understanding. Now it is time to apply your observation skills to a task more like those you will be engaged in throughout the remainder of this text. To increase your cultural understanding and to benefit fully from observation, you, of course, need to observe real behavior outside your classroom.

To begin, though, we will not ask you to venture too far from the context with which you are already familiar and comfortable. Your first "natural" observation task will take you to a class in which you are not enrolled as a student. Your goal is to describe people's behaviors as they teach and learn in this classroom.

LEARNING STRATEGY

Managing Your Learning: Reviewing observation checklists enhances your observation skills.

PREPARING FOR YOUR OBSERVATION

Arrange to observe a class at your school. Your teacher can give you some advice on whom to ask for permission. When you ask for permission, explain that your purpose for observing the class is to increase your understanding of how a classroom functions.

As you make your plans, be aware that you must stay for the entire class period to get a full understanding of the class. (You might also violate a rule of classroom behavior by leaving early.)

NOTE: As you prepare for your observation, consult the Observation Checklist on page 51. This checklist also appears in Appendix B so you may refer to it as you complete other observation tasks throughout the text.

OBSERVATION CHECKLIST

_____ Did I receive permission, if permission is necessary, to observe?

_____ Did I prepare for the observation? Did I think about what I might see and hear? For example:

   _____ Where will I observe this behavior?

   _____ What activities do I expect to see?

   _____ Whom do I expect to see?

   _____ What do I expect them to say?

   _____ What do I expect to be their reasons for participating in this behavior?

_____ Am I at the observation site a few minutes before I am to begin my observation? Did I bring several sheets of paper and a good pen?

_____ Am I sitting or standing in a place where I can observe, but not interfere with, all activities?

_____ Am I taking notes on everything I observe?

_____ Am I observing both what is happening and how it is happening?

_____ Am I writing down just the things I see happening?

_____ Am I recording enough evidence to support any assumptions or inferences I will be making?

LEARNING STRATEGY

Overcoming Limitations: Class observation increases your understanding of appropriate classroom behavior.

CONTRIBUTE YOUR IDEAS

You need to ask permission before observing. What would you say to a teacher to explain your task?

1. With another student, write a dialogue between yourself and a teacher explaining what you need to do and asking permission to do it.
2. Practice your dialogue briefly, and role-play it for the rest of the class.
3. As you listen to the dialogues, write down the phrases you think are the most appropriate for explaining your task and asking permission.

OBSERVATION TASK

Classroom Teaching and Learning

Following the BEHAVIOR model, observe and record the classroom teaching and learning behaviors.

IT WORKS!
Learning Strategy:
Reflecting on
Your Experience

JOURNAL

Evaluating Observation

What is your reaction to your observation experience? Do you think your observations and analysis increased your understanding of teaching and learning behavior in the contact culture classroom? Did you enjoy observing?

LEARNING STRATEGY

Understanding and Using Emotions: Being aware of your feelings improves your observation.

CONTRIBUTE YOUR IDEAS

Compare your observation experience with your classmates' experiences.

1. Did you or your classmates face any difficulties while observing? Do you or your classmates have any questions about the observation process or the BEHAVIOR model?
2. Review your observation notes and the results of your analysis. How do your findings about classroom teaching and learning behavior compare with your classmates'?
3. How does your analysis of your own classroom compare to your analysis of another classroom? Were any of the ingredients of teaching and learning behavior described similarly? Which ingredients were described differently?

LEARNING STRATEGY

Testing Hypotheses: Comparing your prior understanding against knowledge you gain through observation enhances your learning.

Threads

The first compulsory school attendance law in the United States stated that children, 8 to 14 years old, must attend school for 12 weeks in the year.

Famous First Facts

TALK IT OVER

List on the blackboard all the rules of teaching and learning behavior you and your classmates identified. Then, discuss the following questions.

1. Which rules appear to be common to all classrooms?
2. Which rules appear to differ from one classroom to another?
3. Why do these similarities and differences exist?
4. Do you believe that any of the rules of teaching and learning you observed are influenced by culture? If so, which ones? How are they influenced?
5. How do the rules of classroom behavior in your contact culture compare to the rules in your native culture?

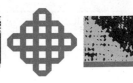

A PUZZLE OF TERMS

Acquiring the skills to observe and understand cultural behavior is a necessary step in the process of increasing your cultural knowledge. Part of this step is learning how to talk about the process. The terms you have been introduced to in this chapter will be useful to you as you conduct your observations and also as you share your increasing cultural understanding with others. To help you review these terms, complete the following word search puzzle. Hidden in the puzzle are the terms you have been introduced to in this chapter. Find the terms and circle them. Make a list of the terms as you find them.

Behavior
Background
Expressions
Hopes
Activities
Values
Individuals
Order
Rules
Contact Culture
Analyze
Description
Observation

```
B W T D L T H S N A L T E R O
A L A O B A B S E P E H O N S
C O W O B S E R V A T I O N X
K V E K E L B A K S E U L V A
G O X R H O P E S R U B E S T
R I P G A J I N R R C L O M A
O P R E V I E V A L U E S O M
U S E D I N B U C I U V B L Y
N D S P O I E S T O I N N U T
D E S C R I P T I O N E D R O
P R I N K O L D V I D E M E L
R U O R D E R R I N I W O R P
E L N O R L U E T D V O P U F
S B S P O E L D I V I I H T C
S D E W D P E L E D D N I L X
H O W E E N S I S U U T G O Z
B L A B R T O N A N A L Y Z E
O C O N T A C T C U L T U R E
H O O V O N C T O L S S N Q J
S N I S O T E S P S S A R A H
```

When you have completed the puzzle, compare it and your list of terms to a classmate's. Did you both find all the terms?

JOURNAL

Reviewing Your Journey

What questions do you have about classroom behavior that you could answer with further observations? List your questions in case you have the opportunity to gather more data on classroom behavior.

THE JOURNEY CONTINUES

We hope that your spirit of adventure has been aroused and that you look forward to continuing your journey to cultural understanding through further observations.

What other cultural behaviors would you like to learn more about? Think about them because in the next chapter you will get your chance!

The Places of Culture

". . . most of what we learn . . . , we don't learn it by being taught. We learn it by looking around, by talking to people, hearing them talk, reading."

–John Holt

5

CHAPTER

"There is a lovely road that runs from Ixopo into the hills. These hills are grass-covered and rolling, and they are lovely beyond any singing of it. The road climbs seven miles into them, to Carisbrooke; and from there, if there is no mist, you look down on one of the fairest valleys of Africa."

–From *Cry, the Beloved Country* by Alan Paton

CONSIDER THIS

Threads

Comiskey Park, home of the Chicago White Sox, was called the Baseball Palace of the world when it opened in 1910.

What places do you have special memories of? Which of these places have significance to you personally? Which of these places are important to you because they have special significance in your culture?

_____

_____

_____

_____

_____

_____

_____

In Chapter 4, you learned that there are various ingredients which together make up a cultural behavior. Among these ingredients is the background or the place where the behavior occurs. This place influences the way the behavior is carried out as well as the meaning the behavior has for the culture and its members.

In this chapter, as you continue to concentrate on increasing your understanding of your contact culture, you will explore behaviors in two distinct places. One of these places will be your college campus where you will study what happens outside the classroom. The other place will be the world outside or off your campus where another similar yet distinct set of rules operates.

5.1 CAMPUS CULTURE

We will focus first on the college or university campus since that is the place where you will be spending most of your time and with which you are probably the most familiar.

Before you read about campus expectations, prepare yourself by learning some of the vocabulary used in the reading.

LANGUAGE FOCUS

Pre-reading Vocabulary

The following questions are designed to help you discover the meaning of new vocabulary words without relying on your dictionary. If you can figure out the meaning of a word by yourself you will be much more likely to remember it, and you will use your time more efficiently. As your skills develop, so will your speed and accuracy.

Work on the following vocabulary questions with a partner. When you have finished, check your answers with another group.

1. Collegial
   a. What other word with similar spelling do you know?
   b. What does it mean?

   EXAMPLE: Tyshon really enjoyed the collegial atmosphere at his university. It was so different from the atmosphere at his high school.

   c. What part of speech is *collegial?*
   d. What do you think it means?

2. Policies
   a. What other words with similar spelling do you know?
   b. What do they mean?

   EXAMPLE: Although the policies of the park district were strict, they helped keep the area safe and clean.

   c. What part of speech is *policies?*
   d. What do you think it means?

3. Ensure
   a. What other words do you know that might be related to this one?
   b. What do they mean?

   EXAMPLE: To ensure that the man would really come back and pay for his dinner, the restaurant owner kept the man's driver's license and his wife.

   c. What part of speech is *ensure?*
   d. What do you think it means?
   e. What does the syllable *en-* mean?

4. Enhance
   a. What part of the word *enhance* do you know?

   EXAMPLE: To enhance her beauty, the woman exercised daily and styled her hair carefully.

   b. What do you think *enhance* means?

5. Engage
   a. What part of the word *engage* do you already know?

   EXAMPLE: To lose weight effectively, a person must eat a low-fat diet and engage in frequent exercise.

   b. What do you think *engage* means?

6. Consistent, Conducive, Contribute, Context
   a. What syllable do these words share?
   b. Which of these words do you already know? What do they mean?
   c. What do you think the syllable *con-* means in these words?
   d. Do you know any words that might be related to the four words above? For example, do you know any other words that have *sist* in them? Do you know any that have *duc* or *tribut* or *text* ? List them.
   e. What do you think each root means? Look them up in a dictionary if necessary.

   sist =
   duc =
   tribu =
   text =

READING

Rights and Responsibilities

When you came to your present college, you probably received a handbook explaining your rights and responsibilities as a student and introducing you to the campus. A handbook is like your guide to the expectations of the university or college. The following excerpt is from the 1989–1990 Student Handbook at Northeastern Illinois University.

The University is a community in which all members are expected to contribute to an environment that is both collegial and conducive to learning. Hence, students have the right to expect an academically focused and personally supportive environment that will facilitate and enhance their education and personal growth. In this context, students are encouraged to express ideas and opinions, to engage in formal and informal activities, and to move freely about the campus in a manner appropriate to a collegial setting.

A community needs ground rules; its members need to know their rights and responsibilities. Consistent with the educational purpose of the University and the recognition of the University as a community, Northeastern Illinois University has adopted policies and procedures to ensure and protect the rights of students and foster the teaching-learning process.

–Student Handbook

CONTRIBUTE YOUR IDEAS

1. What is the message of the first paragraph? In your own words, briefly explain its meaning.

2. What was the main idea of the second paragraph?

3. Compare your answers with those of two or three other students. Do you have the same ideas? Discuss your answers.

TALK IT OVER

The university is a community—a community with rules. The university, then, is a culture. Like all cultures, the university is filled with individuals who have similar hopes and who participate in similar activities. And, as the statement from the Student Handbook makes clear, these individuals are ensured certain rights.

1. What rights do you believe college or university students have? In other words, what can students expect their school to do for them?

2. What expectations do you have of your college or university? What do you expect to learn? What do you expect of your teachers?

3. As the Student Handbook says, along with your rights, you have certain responsibilities as a student. Some of these are written rules and others are simply understood. These include behaviors like being quiet in the library, putting trash in the garbage can, not writing on walls and desks, and treating fellow students with respect. What are some of the rules at your college that you need to follow to behave appropriately? List as many as you can.

Campus Activities

Some of the rules on your campus are probably quite familiar to you. There are probably others that you know nothing about. This may be because you have never been involved in the activities those rules govern or simply because you haven't learned the rules yet.

So that you may become more familiar with campus behaviors and rules, focus on behaviors and activities that take place at your school. Walk around your campus noticing places and people and looking at bulletin boards where information about campus activities is publicized. These announcements and your casual observations will give you an idea of behaviors that take place at your school. Make a list of the things you see happening, places where things happen, and the announcements that you find.

Sample list:

1. Students studying in the cafeteria
2. A meeting of the Law Students' Club
3. The reference librarian helping someone
4. Students in line at the parking office

Threads

Before the Civil War, 183 permanent colleges and universities which maintained existence until at least 1932, were founded in the United States.

American Education
Its Men, Ideas, and Institutions

1. With three or four classmates, make a combined list of the behaviors or activities you have seen at your school that you would like to understand better. Choose one member of your group to write your group's list on the blackboard. After each group's list is on the blackboard, study them.
2. Choose the one behavior or activity you are most interested in better understanding. Write your name on the blackboard next to it.
3. When everyone has chosen a behavior, form groups of students who have chosen the same behavior. If only one student's name appears beside a behavior, that student should choose another behavior that at least one other student has chosen. Keep the groups limited to three or four students.

Managing Your Learning: Planning allows you to focus your observations.

PREPARING FOR YOUR OBSERVATION

With your group, plan your observation of the behavior you have chosen.

1. Talk about the behavior. Why did you choose to observe it? What about it interests you? What do you know about the behavior already? What else would you like to know? Where on campus can you observe this behavior?
2. Guess which individual behaviors may be parts of the larger behavior or activity. Decide which ones you want to focus on or if each person wants to take a different one.
3. Because all group members must observe at the same time, plan a time and place to meet to conduct your observations.
4. Review the Observation Checklist in Appendix B.

OBSERVATION TASK

Campus Behavior

1. Conduct your observation. Use the BEHAVIOR model and the Observation Questions in Appendix A to structure your observation.
2. Make a note of any materials or objects used by the individuals as they engage in the behavior. Gather samples of these materials if you can, as they are a good accompaniment to your notes. These objects could be programs, agendas, banners, or even cups.
3. If possible, take a photograph of the behavior as it is occurring. Be sure to get permission if necessary.

CONTRIBUTE YOUR IDEAS

IT WORKS!
Learning Strategy:
Considering Your
Feelings

Within your group, discuss your feelings about your observation experience. Did you enjoy observing with the BEHAVIOR model? What is your reaction to the behavior you observed?

5.3 ANALYZING CAMPUS CULTURE

LEARNING STRATEGY

Remembering New Material: Demonstrating the behavior you observed helps you recall and relate what you learned.

Demonstrate the Behavior

Inform your classmates of what you learned through your observation. Rather than simply retell your experience, however, present your findings in one or a combination of the following ways:

- role-play
- write and recite a poem
- write and sing a song
- draw a picture or series of pictures

As you demonstrate the behavior, try to behave as the individuals you observed behaved. Say what they said, move as they moved, and, if possible, use materials that they used. If you have photographs of the behavior as you observed it, share them with the class.

LEARNING STRATEGY

Forming Concepts: By analyzing physical materials you can infer their function in and value to their culture.

CONTRIBUTE YOUR IDEAS

Focus on the materials gathered during your classmates' observations. Review the behavior associated with the materials that were collected. Then, as an anthropologist would, analyze the materials as cultural artifacts.

What can you infer about the individuals who use the artifact from the shape, function, and content of the artifact?

For example, if the artifact is a program of scheduled business for a particular meeting, we could infer that this culture values time, accomplishment, organization, and planning. We could assume that people at the meeting can read and want to know what will take place before it actually happens. If many of the programs were thrown away or left at the end of the meeting, we can assume that the schedule no longer matters, that it was important or useful only before each item of business took place. If it is nicely typed on good paper, perhaps we will guess that the appearance of the program matters to people of this culture.

TALK IT OVER

1. On the blackboard create a chart like the one below for each of the behaviors observed by your classmates. At the top of each column, write the name of the behavior.
2. Review what you learned about each behavior through the demonstration and artifact tasks.
3. As a class, identify the rules that individuals follow in the performance of each behavior. Have one class member fill in the chart on the blackboard as the rest of you copy the information in your notebook.

	BEHAVIOR	BEHAVIOR	BEHAVIOR	BEHAVIOR
RULE 1				
RULE 2				
RULE 3				
RULE 4				
VALUES				

LEARNING STRATEGY

Forming Concepts: Draw conclusions by inferring the meaning of observed behavior.

CHECKPOINT

The rules that govern the behaviors you observed explain <u>how</u> the behavior is carried out. Understanding cultural behavior, however, involves more than understanding the rules of behavior.

You also need to understand the reasons the behavior occurs. <u>Why</u> do members of the culture engage in these behaviors? Why are these behaviors important in your contact culture? What cultural values do they reflect?

CONTRIBUTE YOUR IDEAS

Look again at the chart. The final line asks you to consider the cultural values associated with the behaviors. On these lines on the blackboard and in your notebook, write the values associated with each behavior. How do the values your group identified compare to the values the other groups chose?

Remembering New Material: Phrasing a value as a proverb provides a useful formula for storing cultural knowledge.

CREATE A PROVERB

Values play an important role in structuring behavior in all cultures. One way individuals show their awareness of a culture's values is through their use of proverbs. Examples of American English proverbs that reflect cultural values are "Time is money," "All's well that ends well," and "Look before you leap."

From the chart, pick two of the values you have identified. With a partner, express each value as a proverb. Record your proverbs in the space below.

1. _____
   _____

2. _____
   _____

Threads

There's more than one way to skin a cat.

OBSERVATION TASK

The Campus in Your Native Culture
Choose one of the behaviors listed in the chart. Using the BEHAVIOR model as a guide, analyze this behavior as it is carried out in your native culture. Make notes on your analysis.

Because you are not in your native culture, you cannot, of course, observe this behavior taking place. Therefore, you will need to call upon what you remember about how this behavior is carried out. If you are unfamiliar with a college campus in your native culture, you may analyze the behavior as you remember seeing it at another educational setting such as a high school in your native culture.

CONTRIBUTE YOUR IDEAS

With a classmate, compare the behaviors investigated on your contact culture campus with the native culture behavior you described above.

1. What rules and values are similar across cultures?
2. Which are different?
3. How do these similarities and differences reflect other similarities and differences that you know exist between these cultures?

Overcoming Limitations: You can compensate for limited knowledge by drawing conclusions from obtainable information.

1. What can you learn about a culture and its members from college behavior?
2. Is college behavior a reflection of behavior in the larger culture? How?

The college campus is only one place in which behaviors governed by cultural rules are displayed. Therefore, college behavior is only one reflection of cultural behavior. If you have not already, in time you will journey off campus. When you do, it will be equally important that you understand the behaviors that occur in this background as well. In the remainder of this chapter, you will investigate some of the places in your community and the behaviors that occur there as you increase your understanding of your contact culture.

5.4 PLACES IN COMMUNITY CULTURE

In essence, the experience of place is one of those things that everyone recognizes but few take the trouble either to analyze or describe. It is easy to comprehend that the plains of Nebraska, the buildings of Times Square, and the Toshugo Shrine at Kikko produce different experiences that are the result of one's being there. There are different types of places, some of them extraordinarily subtle in their influence.

–E. T. Hall, *An Anthropology of Everyday Life*

Getting to know the community in which you live takes some time and effort. Newcomers probably find the grocery store and bank first. Then, as needed, they find other places, such as the post office, library, dentist's office, or movie theater. Eventually, if they choose, they become members of the community, participating in its events and interacting with its other members.

CONSIDER THIS

What places have you been to in your contact culture that do not exist in your native culture? Do you think these places are unique to your contact culture? If so, why?

_____

_____

_____

_____

_____

_____

_____

IDENTIFY IMPORTANT PLACES IN YOUR COMMUNITY

1. List all the places where people of your community gather for social, political, educational, religious, or leisure activities.

   HINT: For ideas, look in the phone book, call the city hall, talk to community residents, walk or drive around the nonresidential areas. When identifying the places, be as specific as possible. For example, in the community you may find eight churches, three synagogues, a public library, the city hall, the community center, a health club, a grocery store, and a park.

2. Write your list of places on a chart similar to the one on the following page. Then write down what kinds of activities you believe happen there. Finally, indicate with a check whether or not you have been to the place.

PLACES IN MY COMMUNITY	WHAT HAPPENS THERE	I HAVE BEEN THERE	I HAVE NOT BEEN THERE
_____	_____	_____	_____
_____	_____	_____	_____
_____	_____	_____	_____
_____	_____	_____	_____

5.5 OBSERVING PLACES AND BEHAVIORS IN THE COMMUNITY

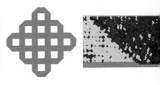

Choose a Place to Observe

Look at your list of places. Choose three you have not been to but are interested in observing.

Call or visit each place to find out a schedule of events for the next week.

Choose one of these events to attend. At some places, such as a playground, there may not be a specific scheduled event to attend. In this case, choose a time when you can observe many people engaged in many behaviors.

NOTE: At each place, in each event, you will see many different cultural behaviors. For example, at a school board meeting (the event) held at a school (the place), there will be behaviors such as greetings, introductions, and discussion of problems. At a playground, you might observe behaviors such as children playing a game, a mother scolding her child, or two children fighting.

Threads

Oh that I were
Where I would be,
Then would I be
Where I am not;
But where I am
There I must be,
And where I would be
I can not.

The Oxford Nursery Rhyme Book

LEARNING STRATEGY

Managing Your Learning: Preparing focuses your observations.

PREPARING FOR YOUR OBSERVATION

To prepare for your observation, first review the Observation Checklist in Appendix B. Then, make a list of expectations you have about the event for each of the ingredients in the BEHAVIOR model. Write down what you think will happen, who you think will be there, how long you think it will last, and so on.

If anyone else in your class has chosen the same event, meet with him/her to discuss how you will conduct your observation. Each of you needs to participate in the observation and analysis of the behaviors, but you may conduct your observation at the same place and time.

OBSERVATION TASK

Observing an Event in Your Community
Conduct your observation and analyze the behaviors using the BEHAVIOR model and the Observation Questions in Appendix A.

LEARNING STRATEGY

Testing Hypotheses: Comparing what you observed to your expectations provides background knowledge for future observations.

TALK IT OVER

How did your observations compare to your expectations? Did they confirm your expectations? Or were your expectations inaccurate?

LEARNING STRATEGY

Personalizing: Viewing a culture through the eyes of its members more closely connects you to the culture.

IF I WERE

How would you explain the meaning that the place where you observed has for members of the culture? Can you explain why this place might be important to members of the culture?

Try to express this meaning by completing the following sentence:

If I were a member of this culture, _____ (the place you observed) would be important for me because

_____

_____

_____

_____

_____

WRITE ABOUT IT

A Cultural Rule Book

People need to be informed of appropriate behaviors and the rules for how to engage in them.

You can have a role in informing others by creating a pamphlet or rule book that identifies the behaviors and rules for the place you observed.

Design your rule book in the following way:

1. On the first page, identify the place and list the events and behaviors one would see in this place.
2. On the next page(s), identify the rules for the behaviors.
3. Then, add a section of advice. What advice would you give to someone who has not been to this place?

NOTE: Remember, when trying to understand a culture other than your own, it is important that you interpret cultural behavior through the eyes of the participants. Try not to allow your native culture to influence your interpretation. Be descriptive rather than judgmental.

READING

Your Classmates' Rule Books

1. Make a copy of your rule book for each of your classmates. They too will copy their rule books for the class.
2. As you read through your classmates' rule books, see if you can identify any rules common to all of the behaviors. Be prepared to discuss your findings in class.

TALK IT OVER

1. If you found similar rules for different behaviors, what does this suggest?
2. If you found different rules for the same behavior, what does this suggest?
3. What cultural values can you identify by looking at the lists of rules compiled by your classmates?

JOURNAL

Reviewing Your Journey

In this chapter, you have learned about the role of place in culture. To you, what is the significance of places in a culture? Illustrate your thoughts in a drawing or through a poem. (Read the following poem for inspiration.)

READING

The Cave

Sometimes when the boy was troubled he would go
   To a little **cave** of stone above the brook
And build a fire just big enough to glow
   Upon the **ledge** outside, then sit and look.
Below him was the winding silver trail
   Of water from the upland pasture **springs,**
And meadows where he heard the calling **quail;**
   Before him was the sky, and passing wings.

The **tang** of willow **twigs** he lighted there,
   Fragrance of meadows breathing slow and deep,
The cave's own **musky** coolness on the air,
   The scent of sunlight . . . all were his to keep.
We had such places—cave or tree or hill . . .
   And we are lucky if we keep them still.

–Glenn W. Dresback

Vocabulary
cave: a hole in a hill
ledge: a shelf
springs: underground sources of water
quail: a small bird
tang: a sharp smell
twigs: small sticks
fragrance: pleasant smell
musky: strong animal smell
scent: smell

THE JOURNEY CONTINUES

In the chapters that follow, you will be introduced to a variety of ways culture is reflected in behaviors and in individuals. In chapters that investigate the people of your contact culture, their language, and their channels of information, you will continue to increase your cultural understanding.

The People of Culture

"*The capacities of mankind, the human species, are very great and very wonderful and have shown themselves in very wonderful accomplishments throughout the ages. For the moment we tend to forget that, because we see things going so badly, so out of control, and, in a sense, so badly managed. . . .*

I want to remind myself that our species does have other capacities and I don't think they've changed."

–Barbara Tuchman

INTRODUCTION

I've conceived this book in the hope that the encounter of one people with another need not always result in collision, that an exchange between even the most different peoples can result in enrichment rather than conflict and exploitation. But this is an era of instant experience and unthinking immediacy. It is assumed that knowing the location and price of a good hotel and having a road map is about all that is needed to get you from here to wherever you want to go. But it is easier to go to the moon than it is to enter the world of another civilization.

–Jamake Highwater

CONSIDER THIS

This passage is taken from the introduction of a travel guide that Jamake Highwater has written for American tourists to "Indian America." In writing his book, what two things did he hope for? Why does he doubt that his hopes will come true? What do you think of his ideas?

_____

_____

_____

_____

_____

_____

In Chapter 5 you explored behaviors that take place on your campus and in your community. You discovered that the place influences both the way a behavior is carried out and the meaning of that particular behavior. In this chapter, you will move beyond the study of place to the study of the people or the individuals of a culture. As Jamake Highwater notes, we need more than a map of the area to understand a culture. We need to have contact with the people.

6.1 INDIVIDUALS AND THEIR CULTURE

Forming Concepts: Understanding the relationship between two concepts is eased when you compare them to concepts whose relationship you understand.

Associate

For Highwater, cultural understanding means more than just watching people in their own cultures. He thinks an understanding of the individuals who create these cultures and participate in these cultures is essential.

One way to explain the relationship between two things is to make an analogy, or comparison, between it and the relationship between two more familiar things. Study the following analogies.

Dark is to night as *light* is to *day.*

A smile is to happiness as *tears* are to *sadness.*

How would you describe the relationship between a culture and its members? Complete the following analogy with a classmate.

People are to culture as _____ is/are to _____ .

CONTRIBUTE YOUR IDEAS

Write your analogy on the blackboard. Take a few minutes to read the others produced by your classmates. Which one of them do you think best expresses the relationship between individuals and their culture?

READING

Literature can often be a window into a culture. As you read the poem by Walt Whitman, concentrate on what it says about the people of the United States.

I Hear America Singing

I hear America singing, the varied **carols** I hear,
Those of mechanics, each one singing his as it should be blithe and
    strong,
The carpenter singing his as he measures his plank or beam,
The mason singing his as he makes ready for work, or leaves off work,
The boatman singing what belongs to him in his boat, the deckhand
    singing on the steamboat deck,
The shoemaker singing as he sits on his bench, the hatter singing as
    he stands,
The wood-cutter's song, the **ploughboy's** on his way in the
    morning, or at noon intermission or at sundown,
The delicious singing of the mother, or of the young wife at work, or
    of the girl sewing or washing,
Each singing what belongs to him or her and none else,
The day what belongs to the day—at night the party of young
    fellows, **robust,** friendly,
Singing with open mouths their strong melodious songs.
                –Walt Whitman

Vocabulary
carols: songs
ploughboy: a boy who digs up the soil in a field to make it ready for planting
robust: strong, powerful, muscular

TALK IT OVER

Obviously, Walt Whitman could not mention every person who lives in America. Instead, he chose to categorize the people of the United States.

1. What categories or groups does he identify?
2. Why do you think he chose these categories?
3. What attitude is expressed in this poem?
4. How does this poem make you feel? What does it make you think about America or Americans?

CHECKPOINT

There are, of course, many ways to categorize people, many ways to label them, and many groups that even one individual can fit into. One way to classify people is by the work they do. Other classifications might be made according to people's lifestyles, beliefs, attitudes, or personalities.

LEARNING STRATEGY

Forming Concepts: Seeing the relationships among individuals helps you recognize their group affiliations.

CONTRIBUTE YOUR IDEAS

1. Walt Whitman grouped Americans by their work, their gender, and their age. With two or three classmates, make a list of other possible ways to group the people in your contact culture. Be as specific as possible. Write your answers in the space below.

_____

_____

_____

_____

2. When you finish making your list, read it again and circle the classifications that are most important to you in defining a person from your contact culture. In other words, which things are most important for you to know about someone from your contact culture whom you are meeting for the first time?

3. If members of your contact culture were to identify or categorize themselves, what adjectives or labels do you think they would use? How do they identify or categorize themselves when introducing each other or themselves? If they are describing a person to someone, which things about the person do they always mention?

4. What categories do you fit into? What labels do you use to define yourself when talking to others?

IT WORKS!
Learning Strategy:
Understanding
Yourself

LEARNING STRATEGY

Testing Hypotheses: Listening to your classmates' opinions helps you evaluate your own.

TALK IT OVER

1. What are the advantages and disadvantages of classifying individuals in a culture? When is it useful? When might it be harmful?

2. How do you feel when someone from another culture classifies the people of your culture?

6.2 THE IMPACT OF STEREOTYPES

LEARNING STRATEGY

Understanding and Using Emotions: Considering your feelings in a particular situation helps you understand other people's feelings in similar situations.

JOURNAL

Experiencing Discrimination

Have you ever experienced discrimination? Do you know someone who has? Describe the situation and the feelings that experience evoked.

CHECKPOINT

A common basis for discrimination (treating certain individuals in a way different from the way you treat others) is called **stereotyping.** When we stereotype, we assign characteristics or labels to all members of a particular group because they are observed in some members of the group. For example, if one red-haired person is seen to get very angry, then all red-haired people are believed to get angry easily. Stereotypes are, obviously, quite often inaccurate.

LISTENING

A Memory

Jamake Highwater became aware of the way stereotypes influence people when he was still young. In the story you will hear, Highwater tells about stereotypes he saw on television when he was a child.

Vocabulary focus: The following words are in Highwater's story. Before listening, match them with their definitions.

1. _____ cavalry   **a.** bad dreams

2. _____ nightmares   **b.** false or fake

3. _____ Max Factor faces   **c.** army on horses

4. _____ phony   **d.** a kind of mask

As your teacher plays the tape, listen to Jamake's experience once. In pairs, talk about the story he tells. Then, in the space below, write the main idea.

_____

_____

_____

_____

Listen to the memory again. Take notes if you wish.

TALK IT OVER

1. What message or stereotype about Native Americans was given in the films?
2. What was this message's impact or influence on Jamake?
3. What impact do you think the films might have had on individuals who are not Native American?
4. Do you think stereotyping is ever useful? Why or why not?

READING

The Consequences of Stereotyping

Read the following letter to the editor of MS Magazine. As you read, consider the consequences of stereotyping that the writer experiences.

I am 16 years old, and an Asian American. . . I was born and grew up in a **predominantly** white community where some children as old as nine or ten hadn't even met a black person or a Native American.

I had to **endure** years of being one of the two "yellow" children in school, **fielding** such questions as "Do Chinese people eat cats?" Little white children called me "chink" and "cheekie-eyed girl," and made fun of my Chinese last name. . .

My parents are **flexible** about who I date, but marriage can become **controversial.** When I told my mom that I might marry a black man she almost had a heart attack. But deep inside I think I want to marry a white man because somehow I think a white man is more chic, and that perhaps he and I would have more in common, since I am saturated with U.S. culture.

[In her article regarding race relations and stereotypes,] Helen Zia wrote, "You can start by trying to talk to the woman next door—or in the next town." It sounds wonderful, but in reality doors are slammed more every day.

-Amy Wu, Thornwood, N.Y.

Vocabulary

predominantly: mainly, mostly
endure: suffer without quitting, experience
fielding: handling, dealing with
flexible: able to change
controversial: able to be argued, debatable

TALK IT OVER

1. What stereotypes has Amy experienced while growing up?
2. Who, in Amy's experience, held these stereotypes?
3. What point is made in the last paragraph?
4. How does the author view the racial situation in the United States?
5. How typical do you think her experiences are?

CONTRIBUTE YOUR IDEAS

List all the stereotypes you have about people in your contact culture. Choose two to write on a slip of paper and give to your teacher. Do not sign your name on the paper.

As your teacher writes all the stereotypes on the board, think about which ones you agree with and which ones you disagree with.

TALK IT OVER

1. Which of the stereotypes are negative and which are positive?
2. Which ones do you believe are true? What support do you have for your conclusions?
3. How do people learn to stereotype? Whom or what does it come from?
4. What impact do your stereotypes of the people in your contact culture have on your cultural adjustment?

JOURNAL

Stereotypes

Stereotyping is a fairly common practice across cultures. What stereotypes do people from other cultures have about people in your culture? Explain how you feel about those stereotypes. Why do you think they exist?

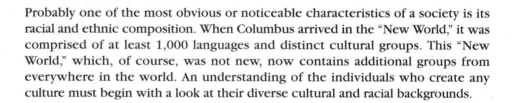

6.3 CULTURAL DIVERSITY

Probably one of the most obvious or noticeable characteristics of a society is its racial and ethnic composition. When Columbus arrived in the "New World," it was comprised of at least 1,000 languages and distinct cultural groups. This "New World," which, of course, was not new, now contains additional groups from everywhere in the world. An understanding of the individuals who create any culture must begin with a look at their diverse cultural and racial backgrounds.

LEARNING STRATEGY

Forming Concepts: Reading charts can help you interpret data.

Let's look at the diversity of the United States.

U.S. POPULATION BY RACE, 1990 CENSUS	
Total population	248,709,873
Non-Hispanic:	
White	188,128,296
Black	29,216,293
American Indian, Eskimo, Aleut	1,793,773
Asian, Pacific Islander	6,968,359
Other race	249,093
Hispanic origin (of any race)	22,354,059

These six groups are classifications of almost innumerable smaller groups, which, if seen in more detail, provide a clearer understanding of the diversity in the United States. Look, for example, at the following list:

**Asian or Pacific Islander Groups Reported
in the 1990 Census**

Asian	**Pacific Islander**
Chinese	Hawaiian
Filipino	Samoan
Japanese	Guamanian
Asian Indian	Other Pacific Islander
Korean	Carolinian
Vietnamese	Fijian
Cambodian	Kosraean
Hmong	Melanesian
Laotian	Micronesian
Thai	Northern Mariana Islander
Other Asian	Palauan
Bangladeshi	Papua New Guinean
Bhutanese	Ponapean
Borneo	Polynesian
Burmese	Solomon Islander
Celebesian	Tahitian
Ceram	Tarawa Islander
Indochinese	Tokelauan
Indonesian	Tongan
Iwo-Jiman	Trukese
Javanese	Yapese
Malayan	Pacific Islander, not specified
Maldivian	
Nepali	
Okinawan	
Pakistani	
Sikkim	
Singaporean	
Sri Lankan	
Sumatran	
Asian, not specified	

CONTRIBUTE YOUR IDEAS

1. In the chart, U.S. Population by Race, the subgroups of the "Hispanic" racial category are not listed. What do you think they are? What subgroups do you think are included in the "Black" racial category? What subgroups are in the "White" category?
2. Consider the racial makeup of your country.
   a. What are the major racial groups?
   b. What subgroups might these major groups contain?
   c. Which group is dominant or has the most power?
   d. Which group or groups lived in your country first?
   e. How have the groups influenced each other over time?

Threads

About 900,000 immigrants enter the United States each year.

Overcoming Limitations: Increase your knowledge of cultural diversity by focusing your observations on your community.

OBSERVATION TASK

Discover the Diversity of Your Neighborhood
Walk around the streets of your neighborhood. Look for signs of the groups of people who live there. Here are some ideas for things to look for:

A. Go into stores, especially grocery stores. Look at the kinds and names of food for sale.

B. Look at newspapers for sale. What languages are they in?

C. Identify the types of religious buildings in your area.

D. What languages do you hear spoken around you?

E. Look through a local street directory. Read the names on your neighbors' mailboxes. Can you identify the ethnic background of your town and of your neighbors?

F. In the local library, are there books in any language besides English?

Threads

Milwaukee was once known as "America's Munich" because of its large German immigrant community.

Midwest Living

SHARE YOUR EXPERIENCE

Tell your classmates about the ethnic makeup of your neighborhood. Describe how and what you learned about your community.

TALK IT OVER

1. Have you ever heard of a culture being called a "melting pot"? What does it mean?
2. Some cultures are described as "salad bowls" or "stews." How do these descriptions differ from "melting pot"?
3. Do you think it is possible for people from different cultures to blend totally with each other as they would in a melting pot?
4. Can peace and harmony exist between ethnically diverse people? Or do the characteristics that make them unique have to disappear first?

JOURNAL

The Blending of Cultures

Using your personal experience, write an answer in your journal to either question 3 or question 4 from the preceding "Talk It Over."

6.4 VOICES OF EXPERIENCE

LISTENING

Perhaps the best voices for determining the effect of cultural diversity are those of experience. Listen to the tape as your teacher plays Anna Quindlen's reflection on her experience with ethnic diversity in the United States.

CONTRIBUTE YOUR IDEAS

1. What are the language skills of each member of the family living next door?
2. Why do you think the family thought it would be better for the son to speak only English?
3. Does Anna believe the United States is a melting pot? Explain.

LEARNING STRATEGY

Testing Hypotheses: Interviewing individuals who have immigrated to your contact culture provides you with information from experts.

Interview

To conclude your investigation of diversity and its role in the lives of the members of a culture, complete the following task which requires you to interview senior members of your contact culture.

I. FIND AN INFORMANT

Find a person to interview. You may work in pairs if you wish, but then you must interview two people.

A. Ideally this person should be a senior citizen, 65 years old or older. This person could be from any ethnic group including yours; however, among the interviewees your class finds, be sure there is a wide variety of backgrounds. The person can be native-born or an immigrant.

B. You can find a senior citizen in a number of places. Talk with a friend's grandparents, a neighbor, or someone in a park. Visit a retirement home, nursing home, or community center near you. Call a senior citizen's service organization listed in your local phone book, explain what you want and ask if they can help. Ask someone from your church, synagogue or temple.

C. Explain that you would like to interview the person to increase your understanding of life and society in your contact culture. Explain that you would like to tape record the conversation so you can listen later for any details you might have missed.

D. Set up a time and place to meet. Plan on at least a half an hour.

II. PREPARE YOUR QUESTIONS

A. Immigrant Informant: Focus on his/her immigration experience.

Ask questions such as

- Where are you from?
- What dreams did you have when you first came to this country?
- Have they come true?
- When did you realize they would/wouldn't?
- Tell me about your experiences as an immigrant or non-native in this country.
- What is your opinion regarding the racial diversity in this country?
- What are the advantages and disadvantages of racial diversity?
- What advice would you give to another person immigrating to this country?

Make up and ask other questions of your own.

B. Native-born Informant:

Ask questions such as

- What is your ethnic heritage?
- How do you think growing up in this country has influenced you?
- What dreams or expectations of life did you have as you were growing up?
- Did these dreams come true?
- When did you realize that you had/had not realized these dreams?
- What is your opinion regarding the racial diversity in this country?

Make up and ask other questions of your own.

NOTES: Find a tape recorder to use to record your interview. Be sure you have batteries since you may not be able to sit near an electrical outlet. Review the Observation Checklist (p.51 or Appendix B).

III. CONDUCT THE INTERVIEW

A. Greet the person, introduce yourself, thank him or her, and explain why you want to do this interview.

B. Turn on the tape recorder right away. Soon both of you will forget that it is there and be less nervous.

C. Your job is simply to ask questions and get the other person to talk as much as possible. You may want to respond to what your informant says, but do not influence his/her thinking. You want your informant's words to be a true reflection of his/her experiences.

As he or she talks, you should participate in the conversation as a serious listener:

- Make eye contact.
- Nod your head when appropriate.
- Say things like "Oh! Uh-huh, Um, Oh really? Why?" etc., when appropriate.

If there is something you aren't clear about or don't understand well, ask about it right away.

D. When you are finished, turn off the recorder and thank the informant.

IV. TRANSCRIBE YOUR DATA

1. Listen to your tape from beginning to end.
2. Write down your questions and the main idea of the person's answer to each one.
3. Choose one part which you find most interesting to transcribe. This could be the answer to one particular question.
4. Transcribe this piece, being careful to put down as precisely as possible the person's exact words.

HOW TO TRANSCRIBE

A. Pick the piece you would like to copy down in writing.

B. Listen to it completely.

C. Rewind the tape, and from the beginning of that section, begin to write down every word that is said. Be precise and exact. You will need to stop the tape and rewind frequently.

D. When you have copied the whole section, go back to the beginning and listen all the way through one more time, editing your script as necessary.

E. For an example, read the following script while your teacher plays the tape of the interview.

The following example of a transcript comes from a September 12, 1992 interview with a Cuban-American woman.

M:—Um—I used to have a heavy accent before. I don't know, do I have an accent now?

I came when I was six and I met J and MB when I was seven or eight and I would see them and they looked so Americanish—so white, so clean, so blue-eyed and I was nothing like that. I was little, I was chubby, I was brown hair, brown eyes, my skin tans in the summertime so I was just a little dark ball hopping around playing and stuff. I never thought I'd fit in.

Interviewer: Do you feel like you fit in now?

M: (Pause) Yeah, I do! I don't know why, but I do! It's wonderful. I guess the more I live here...I feel very American. I feel like if—um—for some reason any countries were fighting and we were forced to fight for a country and even though I was born in Cuba and I still have family there and I can remember some things, the country I would fight for would be the United States. The one country I would want to preserve.

READING

Experiences with Diversity

Provide each of your classmates with a copy of your transcript. For homework, read the transcripts you received and reflect on the experiences and attitudes expressed.

JOURNAL

Evaluating Experience

Write a reaction to one or more of the transcripts that you read. Did you understand the feelings the informant talked about? What understanding of your contact culture have you gained? Did any of the informants have attitudes that were opposite from the attitudes of other informants? How do you account for the difference?

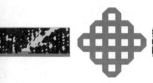

6.5 PRESENTING YOUR RESEARCH

As a class, discuss the two following options for presenting the information you have collected. Decide whether the report or the panel discussion better fits your personal style, and consider which one would better present your information. You could all choose the same form of presentation, or you could use a combination of the two.

PANEL DISCUSSION

Definition

A panel discussion involves a group of people gathered formally to discuss a particular issue. The discussion is guided by a moderator, someone who presents questions but is not otherwise involved in the discussion.

Purpose

The purpose of a panel discussion is to present varied opinions on a topic, thus presenting to the audience the many aspects influencing the issue. Your discussion will encourage expression of the different perspectives held by your informants.

Instructions

Identify the four or five students who will be panelists. Panelists will review their interview information thoroughly, trying to get a clear understanding of their informants' attitudes, opinions, and experiences. Panelists will need to feel comfortable enough with the information so they can answer any questions in the way their informants would. Another student will prepare to be the moderator of the discussion, reviewing the questions to ask and planning the discussion. The questions asked during the panel discussion will be the same as those asked during the interviews.

Threads

Teaching of others, teacheth the teacher.

Procedure

Panelists sit in a semicircle or a row facing the audience. The moderator sits facing the panelists or off to one side. The moderator introduces each panelist as if he or she is the informant. For example, Cheul So Kim will be introduced as Michael Samuelson, the person whom Cheul So Kim interviewed. Cheul So Kim will then answer the questions according to how he thinks Mr. Samuelson would, using the information obtained in the interview. During the discussion, Cheul So Kim will be referred to as Mr. Samuelson by the moderator and the other panelists. Each person wears a name tag, since the names may be difficult to remember.

The moderator guides the discussion, beginning with a brief explanation of the purpose of the discussion and an introduction of each member of the panel. The moderator begins the discussion by asking each of the panelists for his or her opinion on the same question. As the panelists answer, new issues or ideas may come up. The moderator can extend the discussion by asking for comments on the new issues and allowing disagreement or discussion among panelists.

REPORTS

Definition

A report is the information gained from a group of two or more informants that is combined and explained formally to the class by a team of students.

Purpose

The goal of these reports is to compare and contrast informants' opinions, experiences, and views and arrive at some conclusions or discoveries about your contact culture.

Instructions

Identify two, three, or four students who will work on their report together. Each student studies the results of the interviews conducted by their group members, looking for contrasts and similarities in opinion or experiences. As a team, the students discuss these similarities and differences, attempting to explain them and analyze them. For example, what general statements can they make about their contact culture? They may prepare a presentation or report in which they present the comparisons and contrasts they found and in which they explain their analyses and conclusions. All the members of their report team should have an equal part in the presentation. If appropriate, they should choose parts of the interview tapes to play during their report as support for their statements.

Procedure
Presenters stand in front of the class to speak. They introduce themselves, identify their informants and provide some background information about them. They report to the class the similarities and contrasts found, explain their conclusions, and play applicable parts of the tapes as examples. The audience asks questions at the end of the presentation.

6.6 REFLECTING ON WHAT YOU HAVE LEARNED

LEARNING STRATEGY

Remembering New Material: Reviewing information you gained through earlier activities prepares you to apply this information to new activities.

TALK IT OVER

Consider the knowledge you have gained in this chapter. Review the ideas discussed earlier and the opinions of the informants as you discuss the following questions.

1. What advantages might a culture have because of its diverse population?
2. What disadvantages might it have?
3. For hundreds of years, immigrants from all over the world have come to your contact culture to start a new life. How do you think these people have affected the development of the culture?
4. How do you think its cultural diversity will affect your contact culture in the future?

JOURNAL

Reviewing Your Journey
How do you feel about cultural diversity? What ideas and beliefs would you teach your children? What would you like them to think about diversity?

THE JOURNEY CONTINUES

Chapter 6 has focused on the relationship of people to culture. We have seen that, to understand a culture, one must understand the diversity in cultural and ethnic heritage that exists within it. Chapter 7 looks again at diversity. However, instead of focusing completely on the individual in society, it considers three social categories that help create the views and values of the members of a culture.

7

CHAPTER

The Society of Culture

"You can observe people. You can hear people without entering into their lives. You can always evaluate people just by their actions, their expressions, what they say or the way they look, the way they act, or what they do, what their pastime is, what their job is, and the way they live and the kind of house they live in and what they do for a living. They reveal themselves as they are."

–Erskine Caldwell

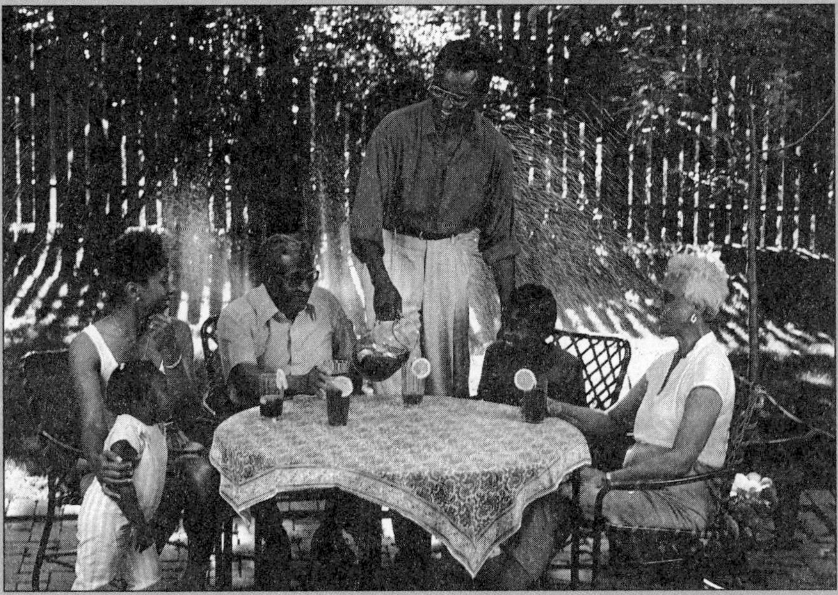

Warning

When I am an old woman I shall wear purple
With a red hat which doesn't go, and doesn't suit me.
And I shall spend my pension on brandy and summer gloves
And satin sandals, and say we've no money for butter.
I shall sit down on the pavement when I'm tired
And gobble up samples in shops and press alarm bells
And run my stick along the public railings
And make up for the sobriety of my youth.
I shall go out in my slippers in the rain
And pick the flowers in other people's gardens
And learn to spit.

You can wear terrible shirts and grow more fat
And eat three pounds of sausages at a go
Or only bread and pickle for a week
And hoard pens and pencils and beermats and things in boxes.

But now we must have clothes that keep us dry
And pay our rent and not swear in the street
And set a good example for the children.
We must have friends to dinner and read the papers.

But maybe I ought to practise a little now?
So people who know me are not too shocked and surprised
When suddenly I am old, and start to wear purple.

–Jenny Joseph

TALK IT OVER

1. What point is the woman trying to make in the first two stanzas?
2. Does she wear purple now? Explain.
3. What does she do now?
4. How does she view old age?
5. How does she view her current age?
6. What do the expectations of her society or culture have to do with her present life?
7. In what ways do the expectations of her society change as a woman ages?

CONSIDER THIS

What is the role of culture in defining what a person does? What is the role of culture in defining how one person views another person's behavior?

_____

_____

_____

Throughout life, a person may be involved in many different relationships. How that person understands those relationships will depend on many things. It may depend on the person's education, gender, age, or position in a family. It may depend on the person's seniority in a job or on the person's race or social class. Since it would be impossible to investigate all of these influences in one chapter, we have chosen to focus on the issues of family, age, and gender and the ways in which these are viewed in a culture.

7.1 THE FAMILY

WRITE ABOUT IT

A child's first understanding of the world and concept of identity almost always begins with his or her family. The caretaker, usually a family member, is the first context the infant has. We recognize our ties to our family early in our lives. In most cultures, we learn to identify ourselves by our names, thus providing the world with information about our familial connections.

In your opinion, what is a family? Give a brief definition below.

_____

_____

_____

Threads

In Iceland there are no family names. Everyone is identified as the son or daughter of his or her father.

Encyclopedia of World Cultures

READING

As you consider your definition of a family, you may find it interesting to read the responses of six people who were asked to define the word "family."

Family Definitions

"Someone or a group that loves you and is there when you need him/her or them."

"People bound by blood or love. Parents may not love their children or vice versa. Other families adopt and no blood but love is there. It's expanded in concept. Two people living together is not family, but if they adopt a child, they're a family. If you have a marriage certificate—you're a family. Marriage equals responsibility for the other person's families."

"Any group of people who care for and about each other beyond the expectation of friendship."

"People who live with you like your mother and father—the immediate family. A group of people you're close to. Whatever an individual considers his/her family."

"I recognize that family units take many forms; however, I see the ideal family as one father, one mother, children, and possibly an intergenerational household."

Forming Concepts: Reading and hearing the views of others can help you form your own ideas and opinions.

TALK IT OVER

1. Which of the previous definitions of family most closely matches the one you created?
2. After reading those definitions, and the ones your classmates wrote, would you like to change your definition in any way?

LISTENING

A "Family" Conversation

While everyone knows intuitively what a family is, it is not that easy to agree on a definition. As your teacher plays the tape, listen to the following conversation between a husband and wife, and an interviewer.

CONTRIBUTE YOUR IDEAS

1. What is this couple's first definition of a family?
2. Are they a family? Explain their discussion of this idea.
3. What examples of "special" families were mentioned?
4. Why do you think it was difficult for this couple to define "family"?

Understanding and Using Emotions: Pictures allow you to represent emotions and relationships visually.

PICTURE THIS

With a group of three or four classmates, discuss the definitions of family that you wrote earlier in this section. Consider the previous definitions you read and listened to. As a group, combine your definitions into a single definition of family.

Draw a picture to represent your definition. In your picture, try to symbolize the emotions, relationships, and responsibilities involved in being a family.

CONTRIBUTE YOUR IDEAS

1. Share your picture and definition of family with your classmates.
2. What characteristics define a family? In other words, which characteristics did all the groups include in their definitions?

TALK IT OVER

According to a recent study, when asked to respond to the question, "Which of the following comes closest to your definition of the family?" members of U.S. culture responded in the following ways:

A group of people related by blood, marriage, or adoption	22%
A group of people living in one household	3%
A group of people who love and care for each other	74%

Mellman & Lazarus, Inc., Washington, D.C., quoted in *Familyhood, Nurturing the Values That Matter,* by Dr. Lee Salk, p. 23

Threads

Historically, Serbian households were extended family homes, consisting of married brothers, their wives and children.

Encyclopedia of World Cultures

1. How do these definitions compare to the earlier definitions?
2. Why do you think most of the people in this survey preferred a definition of family that centers on love and care rather than on biological relatedness?
3. What advantages and disadvantages might there be for a culture that maintains this definition of family?
4. What advantages and disadvantages might there be for a culture that focuses its definition of family on biological relatedness?

RESEARCH

The concept of family is very important in most cultures. There are, however, as you have read, many definitions of family. To increase your awareness of the place of family in your contact culture, conduct some research on your own.

In class, talk over some of the possible topics that you could research. There are many, so you need to narrow your interest.

Go to the library and find two articles related to your topic in newspapers or magazines. Copy them and take them home to read. If you are unfamiliar with library research, consult a reference librarian for help finding articles.

REPORT

Choose one of the articles to report on to your class. In your report, be sure to explain the focus or purpose of the article and present what you learned about the family in your contact culture. If the article mentions any changes that have taken place in the structure or meaning of the family, discuss those changes and the reasons given for them.

JOURNAL

The Ideal Family
What have you learned about families? In your opinion, what would the ideal family be like?

7.2 THE SIGNIFICANCE OF AGE

In considering the characteristics of the family and its role in culture, the issue of age is often quite important. Our understanding of how a person fits into a family often depends upon the person's age. To begin thinking about the significance of age in a culture, read the following statistics.

> Every day in the United States 6,000 Americans celebrate their 65th birthday and 3,800 Americans celebrate their 75th birthday.
>
> U.S. Bureau of the Census,
> *Projection of the Population,* 1989, p. 43

> America's seniors (individuals over 65) now outnumber the entire population of Canada.
> *Fact Book on Aging,* Elizabeth Vierck, 1990

> An estimate of the number of Americans over 100 years of age ranges from 25,000 to 46,000.
>
> U.S. Bureau of the Census,
> *Centenarians,* 1987, p. 1

Threads

Years ago we discovered the exact dead center of middle age. It occurs when you are too young to take up golf and too old to rush up to the net.

Nods and Becks

TALK IT OVER

1. At what age do you consider a person to be old?
2. Why do you pick that age rather than an earlier or later one?
3. Besides identifying someone as "old," what other adjectives or labels are used for people in this age group?
4. What responsibilities toward younger generations does an elderly person have? What should the elderly do for younger generations?
5. What obligations does a son or daughter have toward an elderly parent? What obligations or responsibilities does a grandchild have?
6. What privileges do elderly people have that they didn't have when they were younger?

LEARNING STRATEGY

Testing Hypotheses: Verify your understanding of your contact culture through interviewing.

INTERVIEW

How do your views on age compare to the views of members of your contact culture?

Ask the questions in "Talk It Over" of a native member of your contact culture. Do his or her views match yours?

READING

People of all ages recognize the differences and divisions between age groups. The following excerpt from an article in *Modern Maturity* quotes letters from older Americans who are writing about the "generation gap"—the sometimes unbridgeable distance between people of different ages.

Empathy can span the abyss

by Malcolm Boyd

Intergenerational conflicts and misunderstandings can cause pain and emotional bruises. Instead of finding rich nurturing and love within the family circle, some people encounter exactly the opposite. (1)

For example, a Nebraska man writes: "I don't look forward to family gatherings because I come back with my self-esteem reduced to zero and feeling like a stereotypical old geezer. I'm rebuffed by my own children, giggled at, and made to feel my thoughts aren't important." (2)

An Indiana reader describes in detail a truly unhappy situation. "I gave my money to my children, trusting them to take care of my needs when I grew older. But now that I have no money left, they have discarded me. How stupid I was not to take care of my security! I'm alone now, really alone. I need to understand what I did wrong. I guess I gave too much, cared too much." (3)

Many letters from elderly people tell similar stories. I also hear from their sons and daughters, members of the so-called sandwich generation, whose reports have a different focus. A 54-year-old woman writes from New York about the "hard burden" she bears in caring for her 88-year-old mother: "I'm angry that I am increasingly having to be a parent to someone whose self-centeredness and narcissism made her unable to be a mother to me. The simple, awful fact is that I respect my mother and love her as my flesh and blood, but I don't like her and I wish she weren't in my life. My fear is that she's going to live on and on, growing more and more needful of my 'parenting,' and that I won't be free of her presence until I'm approaching 70 myself." (4)

Another letter from a member of the sandwich generation comes from Arizona: "My challenge involves my relationship with my mother-in-law of 29 years. She's 89. She has lost all semblance of a positive outlook. She speaks only of her aches and pains and the bleakness of her life. I cannot deal with this negative approach to living. Whatever I try to do for her, nothing is ever right." (5)

LANGUAGE FOCUS

Vocabulary

In the identified paragraph, find the words whose meanings match the definitions given.

In paragraph 1

   a. between people of different ages: _____

   b. arguments, troubles: _____

   c. find, come into contact with: _____

In paragraph 2

    d. elderly man: _____

    e. rejected, given no attention: _____

In paragraph 3

    f. thrown away: _____

    g. future safety: _____

In paragraph 4

    h. stuck between two, in the middle: _____

    i. loving only oneself: _____

    j. relative (three words): _____

In paragraph 5

    k. appearance, likeness, similarity: _____

    l. emptiness, dullness: _____

Comprehension Questions

Answer the following questions about the reading in your own words. Look back to the text if you need to, but do not copy sentences from the text to answer the questions. Think about the meaning in the text and write down your ideas in answer to each question.

1. What problem did the man from Nebraska have?
2. How does the Indianan feel? What happened to him or her?
3. Describe the situation of the 54-year-old woman from New York. Why does she feel angry?
4. The woman from Arizona says she faces a challenge. What does she mean? What is her trouble?

LEARNING STRATEGY

Understanding and Using Emotions: Sharing your advice helps you consider your feelings about a problem.

CONTRIBUTE YOUR IDEAS

In the article, four different problems associated with age differences, or intergenerational conflict, are presented.

A. With another student, choose one of the problems and talk about how the issue could be resolved.

B. Compose a letter to the writer, giving any solutions you may have to his or her complaints.

Having examined the family in your contact culture and the effect age has on a person's role in society, you will next investigate gender and how a person's gender influences his or her role in a culture.

JOURNAL

Male/Female Roles

What do you believe are the typical male and female roles in your contact culture? Draw on what you have observed and heard about gender-based expectations and responsibilities.

How is a male expected to behave? A female?

Are members of each gender responsible for certain duties? If so, which duties?

LANGUAGE FOCUS

Prereading Vocabulary

The following activity focuses on vocabulary you will find in the coming reading. To familiarize yourself with the meanings, match the following words from the text with the best definition.

1. _____ unique
2. _____ pursue
3. _____ shattered
4. _____ breadwinner
5. _____ abuse
6. _____ intransigent
7. _____ ulterior motives
8. _____ sexism
9. _____ validating
10. _____ role model
11. _____ reinforces
12. _____ assume

a. take for granted, automatically believe

b. discrimination in career choices based on a person's gender

c. one of a kind, different from all others

d. showing to be true, proving

e. broken into pieces, destroyed

f. supports, upholds, gives extra strength

g. follow after, try to catch or get

h. physically or psychologically harmful treatment

i. person who earns a family's main income

j. an example, a person to be like or imitate

k. stubborn, unmovable, firm

l. secret reasons

READING

As you read the following article, concentrate on what it reveals about popular beliefs concerning male and female roles.

See Jack . . . teach kindergarten?

by Cindy Schreuder

Room 1 in North Chicago's Yeager Elementary School is a typical kindergarten classroom, with 29 children playing games, singing songs, and teasing each other. In the center of the maelstrom is John Beausoleil, 39, a veteran of 15 years in the kindergarten trenches. (1)

Ask the children if they find the mustachioed man an unlikely teacher and they do not understand. (2)

"He's kind and he's nice," said Joshua Hearn, five. (3)

Most adults have a different reaction. (4)

"Elementary education is not thought of as a man's profession, and kindergarten is even more unusual," Beausoleil said. "But I think it's unique. I'm proud of what I do, so I just come right out and tell people I teach kindergarten." (5)

Few men can say that. (6)

Only about three dozen of the more than 4,000 kindergarten teachers in Illinois are men. And the job isn't attracting many new recruits. (7)

The number of male teachers in kindergarten and other elementary grades nationwide fell this year to its lowest point in a quarter century, according to the National Education Association in Washington. Just 12 percent of the nation's 1.4 million elementary school-teachers are men, the Washington-based NEA says. (8)

That figure is down from a 1981 high of nearly 18 percent nationwide. Comparable figures for Illinois are not readily available. (9)

Education experts say the teaching of young children—neither a high-paying nor a high-status job—is regarded even less favorably during a recession. (10)

"In economic downturns, the money issues become even more pressing for people," said Barbara Willer, public affairs director for the National Association for the Education of Young Children, based in Washington. "The pay [for kindergarten teachers] is so low, it's difficult to attract people." (11)

While women have shattered stereotypes and moved into male-dominated professions such as medicine, law and business, men have been slow to do the reverse and pursue female-dominated careers. (12)

"We're so in tune to being the heads of households and being the breadwinner, and the education field just doesn't pay what other sectors do," said Ronald Whitmore, a kindergarten teacher at Orrington Elementary School in Skokie. (13)

Beyond the issue of economics, however, lies a more intransigent reason: Teaching young children cuts to the core of society's gender roles.

People are accustomed to seeing women working with young children, but men who do the same are viewed as suspicious characters who may harbor ulterior motives. (14)

"I've bumped into that suspicion, and I think all teachers have to be pretty careful now," said Robert Holthusen, a kindergarten teacher in Champaign, speaking of public concerns about child abuse. (15)

"If someone needs a hug, the teacher is there to give the child a hug. I do that. A female teacher would do that," he said. "But both sexes have to be more careful these days than we were a while ago." (16)

To allay parental fears and to ensure that abused children are heard, the concern over possible child abuse is not all bad, he added. But it can be unsettling. (17)

Last year, for example, the mother of a girl in his kindergarten class volunteered in the school two days a week. She later confided to Holthusen that she volunteered so often because she was wary of her daughter's male teacher. (18)

"When she walked in the door and saw who the teacher of her baby girl was going to be, she was skeptical, she told me," Holthusen said. (19)

As the year passed, the woman became comfortable having Holthusen teach her child, he said, and the two eventually became friends. (20)

"She saw I was nurturing, I was protective, and I would ensure they were safe and had a quality education," he said. (21)

That is not a view that society at large holds, psychologists say. (22)

"I don't think there's a lot of support for helping men see it as a career option because of sexism," said James O'Neil, professor of family studies at the University of Connecticut at Storrs. "I think it takes a special man who believes that working with children is very important work and is able to not be so concerned about validating his masculinity." (23)

Male teachers disagree over the extent to which gender differences in teaching styles exist. Some men say they encourage more active play in the classroom than do their female counterparts. (24)

"I think I realize how children, especially males, need the physical side of the activities," said Harrison Jackson, a kindergarten teacher at Edward White School in Chicago. "It's very hard for them to sit quite as long, and often you have to have some very energetic activities, but make them learning activities." (25)

But other male teachers disagree. (26)

"I didn't invent the wheel," said Whitmore, the Skokie teacher. "One thing about teachers is, we steal a lot from each other." (27)

Male teachers do agree that they serve as role models for youngsters. Most male teachers can cite many examples of single mothers who have expressed delight upon seeing a man in the classroom. African-American teachers, in particular, say they act as positive role models for the young black boys in their classes. (28)

"Statistics say that I should be in jail or dead or have a record or be doing something in business or whatever, and this is the last place I should be," said Whitmore, who is black. "For African-American boys, I'm somebody they can be like. For all children I'm saying. . . 'Hey, you can make it.'" (29)

Certainly not all fathers are absent. But even those who are a major presence in their children's lives may be reluctant to participate in the classroom, particularly in the early grades. Male kindergarten teachers say they may be better able to draw fathers out. (30)

"I have fathers who volunteer to go on trips and I think one of the reasons they will go is because I'm going—it's not just going to be all ladies on the trip," Jackson said. (31)

Growing accustomed to being around women is part of the job for male kindergarten teachers. Some say they give it little thought because it is an accepted part of the routine. Other men say it reinforces the idea that they are special. (32)

"I kind of liked being something of a minority," said Roger Valente, who taught kindergarten for seven years before switching to first grade last year. (33)

"I kind of gloried in it a bit. Why? I guess because I always, somewhere inside, considered myself just a little bit of a rebel. I tend to like doing things that are not necessarily the norm," said Valente, who teaches at Walker Elementary School in Skokie. (34)

"Doing this job tended to feed a certain part of that within me," he said. "I enjoyed those looks when people would say, 'You teach kindergarten? How can you teach kindergarten?'" (35)

Superintendents are more likely to assume that male kindergarten teachers will one day find their way out of the classroom and into the school administrative office, male teachers say. It is an assumption that angers some. (36)

"There's sort of the conclusion if you're a man, the only way to improve yourself is to get out of the classroom," Beausoleil said. (37)

Beausoleil, who is beginning his 15th year as a kindergarten teacher, prefers the classroom, playing his guitar as children sing vocabulary-building songs and clapping his hands to help them learn to count. (38)

"I don't feel I became a teacher to become an administrator. I became a teacher because I like teaching," Beausoleil said. "I'm just not ready to quit teaching. I still enjoy seeing the progress children make." (39)

It is that progress that male kindergarten teachers say keeps them in the profession, despite society's doubts. (40)

"You don't make a lot of money, but it's such an opportunity," said Holthusen, the Champaign kindergarten teacher. "When I can see a shy, retiring child come into my room on Sept. 1, and on June 1 this kid gives me a salute and says, 'See you next year, Mr. Holthusen'. . . that still puts goose bumps on my arm." (41)

Chicago Tribune, Oct. 9, 1992

LANGUAGE FOCUS

Idioms

Find each idiomatic expression in the following list in the previous article. (The numbers in parentheses refer to the paragraph numbers shown at the end of each paragraph in the article.) Read the surrounding text. What do you think the phrase means? Discuss your ideas with your classmates.

in tune to (13)
cuts to the core (14)
invent the wheel (27)
to have a record (29)
to get (have) goose bumps (41)

Draw a picture to represent each expression. Below your sketch, describe a circumstance in which you could use the expression.

CONTRIBUTE YOUR IDEAS

1. Who is the article about? Why did Cindy Schreuder report about them?
2. Why are there so few men teaching in elementary schools? Give at least three reasons.
3. What is the main point of paragraphs 14–21? How does the story in paragraphs 18–21 affect your understanding of the problem? In other words, why did the writer include it?
4. What advantages do male teachers bring to their students and school?
5. Why does Roger Valente enjoy teaching kindergarten?
6. Why does Robert Holthusen stay at his job?
7. What does this article reflect about gender roles in the United States? Look through the article to find phrases or words that indicate gender roles. Make three lists for your phrases or words: the first for phrases discussing male elementary school teachers; the second for typical male roles; and the third for female roles.
8. According to the data you collected in question 7, what are men generally expected to be like? What are women generally expected to be like?

LEARNING STRATEGY

Forming Concepts: Evaluating statistical information provides a basis for inferencing.

INTERPRET

The differences that exist in gender expectations and roles also apply to the way men and women are treated in the workplace. Consider the following statistics:

Relationship Between Median Income and Gender
(AGES 25-34)

Diane Hertz, "Employment Characteristics of Older Women," *Monthly Labor Review*, Sept. 1988, Table 3.

1. What does "median income" mean?
2. Why do you think these differences in median income exist?
3. According to the data, what can you conclude about how the business culture of the United States views men as compared to how it views women?

One way to learn about the role of age, gender, and family in culture is through articles and statistics. Another way is to find out first-hand from individuals in the culture.

LEARNING STRATEGY

Managing Your Learning: Summarizing helps you review what you have learned.

WRITE ABOUT IT

Listed below are the topics discussed in this chapter. In the spaces, briefly restate or summarize what you learned about each topic.

FAMILY

_____
_____
_____
_____

AGE

_____
_____
_____
_____

GENDER ROLES

_____
_____
_____
_____

Threads

By the time a man realizes that maybe his father was right, he usually has a son who thinks he's wrong.

Charles Wadsworth

LEARNING STRATEGY

Remembering New Material: Writing down the questions you want to ask helps you recall them during your interview.

PREPARING FOR YOUR INTERVIEW

Now, for each topic, write at least three questions that you would like to ask a member of your contact culture.

Write open-ended questions because they allow your informant to present his or her own views. You do not want to ask closed-ended questions that direct or limit the response. Rather, you want your questions to create windows into your informant's experiences. Study the following examples.

Open-ended questions:
- Who's in a family?
- Into what ages or age categories would you divide life?

Closed-ended questions:
- Do families always contain parents and children?
- Is a 55-year-old middle-aged or old?

NOTE: Always ask your informant to explain his or her answers.

FAMILY

1. _____

_____

2. _____

_____

3. _____

_____

AGE

1. _____

_____

2. _____

_____

3. _____

_____

GENDER

1. _____

_____

2. _____

_____

3. _____

_____

CONTRIBUTE YOUR IDEAS

Share your questions with three or four of your classmates. With your classmates, decide upon one set of 10 to 15 questions to be used as you conduct your interviews.

OBSERVATION TASK

Interview

Using the questions generated in class, interview a member of your contact culture. Note your informant's approximate age and gender and ask about his or her ethnic background.

As the informant talks, try to write down as much as possible of what he or she says. It is not necessary to record every word, but be sure to record the main ideas correctly. Quickly review your notes at the end of the interview so you may clarify or check any responses you are unsure of with your informant.

*IT WORKS!
Learning Strategy:
Increasing Your
Understanding of
Your Contact
Culture*

WRITE ABOUT IT

Write a summary of your interview. First, identify the age, gender, and ethnic background of your informant. Then explain the main points of information your informant shared with you.

SHARE YOUR EXPERIENCE

Distribute a copy of your summaries to each of your classmates. In class or as homework, read each of the summaries and discuss the following questions.

1. Compare the answers to each of the questions in the interviews. What seems to be the most common answer to each question? What explanations can you give for answers that vary?
2. List the beliefs that the informants shared.
3. What advantages do you see in these shared beliefs?
4. Do you see any disadvantages?

PUBLISH

As a class, combine your summaries into a book. Include the transcripts you produced in Chapter 5.

Based on the content of the material in your book, write an introduction to the book that explains your view of the issues of family, age, and gender in the culture.

JOURNAL

Reviewing Your Journey
1. How do you think a person's native culture influences his opinions of other people?
2. How will the knowledge you gained in this chapter affect your relationships with the members of your contact culture?

THE JOURNEY CONTINUES

Through the activities in this chapter, you have seen how individual members of your contact culture are both diverse and united in their experiences and opinions. In Chapters 8 and 9, you will continue to explore the place and form of diversity and uniformity in culture as you focus on the place and function of language in culture.

The Language of Culture

8

CHAPTER

"We held an oxymoron contest and invited listeners to send in samples of contradictions in terms. The examples we gave: jumbo shrimp, airline food, military intelligence, instant coffee. Listeners' responses: funeral party, British passion, remarkably dull, dreadfully plain, pretty ugly, perfect mess, good grief, bad luck, civil war, still life, good morning, drip-dry, typewritten, self-service, postal service, married life.

–Susan Stamberg

In September 1987, I was asked to introduce His Holiness Pope John Paul II, who was to **preside over** a papal mass in Sun Devil Stadium, Tempe, Arizona.

I was humbled by the honor and wanted desperately to do something special. I decided to welcome him in Polish, his native tongue.

The only Pole I knew was a seamstress who did alterations for me from time to time, so I said to her, "Tell me how to welcome the Pope in his own language."

On the night before his arrival, I rehearsed the speech before a couple of priests in charge of the event. I took a deep breath before my big finish, "Arizona vita oitsa sven-tego yana pavwa druu-uuugeggo."

One of the priests said to me, "Why would you want to tell the Pope his luggage is lost?"

I am not good with language.

–Erma Bombeck, *When You Look Like Your Passport Photo,*
It's Time to Go Home

preside over: lead

CONSIDER THIS

For Erma Bombeck, being "good with language" includes having the ability to pronounce the words correctly. What does being "good with language" mean to you? What knowledge of language and what language skills does someone need to have to be good with language?

_____

_____

_____

_____

_____

LEARNING STRATEGY

Understanding and Using Emotions: Considering how amusing language can be heightens your enjoyment of the language.

TALK IT OVER

Today, Erma Bombeck can look back with humor on her experience with Polish. Like Erma, most people learning another language will occasionally err when trying to use that language.

1. Do you remember a time in your study of English when you made a humorous error? Describe the situation.
2. How did you realize you had erred?
3. How did the people who heard your error react?
4. What was the source of your error? Why was it seen as humorous?

Language is clearly a medium through which culture is expressed. Sometimes the words we use tie us to a particular group of people. Sometimes our language separates us from others. This chapter looks at some of the ways that language identifies us as members of a culture.

8.1 THE ROLE OF LANGUAGE IN CULTURE

Often bilingual speakers come across a concept that cannot easily be translated from one language to another. Understanding the concept requires cultural knowledge—perhaps even an understanding of that culture's worldview. Read the example below of a Chinese concept that is difficult to translate into English.

A Chinese Concept

Some people find it difficult to explain the meaning of the following Chinese phrase:

人來就好，何必這麼客氣

The phrase can be used by Taiwanese speakers in the context of refusing things such as help, a gift, hospitality, or a compliment.

It is a polite way to say "There is NO NEED for you to give me this gift." Then it is quite acceptable to receive the gift and not refuse it entirely.

It may be difficult for Taiwanese second language learners to become familiar with all the appropriate contexts in which this phrase can be used.

1. Think of a concept in your language that is difficult to translate into English. Use the space below and write it in your native language.

_____

_____

2. Show your concept to a classmate and try to explain its meaning in English.

TALK IT OVER

1. How successful were you in explaining the concept to your classmate?
2. What cultural knowledge is necessary to understand this concept?
3. How does this concept reflect your native culture's worldview?

READING

A Different Current

The following excerpt describes the frustration of trying to express meaning in another language. As you read it, think about your own experience.

> I'll try to give the story in your language. It's hard to express the way I feel in it, but I don't feel the pain so much when I talk about it in your language. My own words carry too much weight. But I always worry when I finish a part, did I say enough? Did I really connect by those words? You see, your language is set for your way of thinking. It's like a different current. The situation I want to explain is set for another current, and that current carries the strong feelings from a different way of thinking. So it's like plugging a lamp into the wrong current. The energy I put into it takes more than it gives out.
>
> –Mohm Phat
>
> (Mohm Phat, a young victim of Cambodia's Khmer Rouge, is recounting her story to her adoptive mother, Gail Sheehy)
> "Spirit of Survival," from *Intercultural Journeys,* p. 143

TALK IT OVER

1. Can you identify with Mohm Phat's frustration?
2. Do you agree that each language is set for a particular way of thinking?
3. What do you do to overcome any limitations of your second language?

Although we may sometimes have difficulty using a language, we know how important language is in our lives. Language is the main way we share our knowledge and thoughts with others. Language is also the main way cultural knowledge is transmitted within a culture and between cultures.

In the activities that follow, you will look at the sounds and the words of language. You will find out that the way the sounds and words of a language are used are very much influenced by one's cultural knowledge and worldview.

Threads

"Kind words can be short and easy to speak, but their echoes are truly endless."

Mother Theresa

8.2 THE SOUNDS WE PRODUCE

LISTENING

"Hello"

As your teacher plays the tape, listen to "Hello" as it is spoken in different languages. Try to identify the language each "Hello" is from.

LISTENING

My Home

1. Often, when we hear languages, we form opinions of them and of their speakers because of the sounds, intonations, and stress patterns used. In a few sentences in your native language, describe your native country to your classmates.

2. Close your eyes as you listen to your class-mates' native languages. What image or picture forms in your mind as you hear each of the languages?

TALK IT OVER

1. Discuss the variety of sounds, intonations, and stress patterns you heard in your classmates' languages. How did each language sound to you?
2. How does English sound to you?

Threads

The sing-song theory holds that human speech grew out of primitive rhythmic dance chants.

8.3 THE ACCENTS WE HEAR

Our attitudes are not limited to other languages and their speakers. We also have opinions about the languages we know and their speakers. Different people may speak the same language with different accents. This means they may pronounce the sounds of the language in different ways. The differences are usually not big enough to cause problems in understanding. The differences, though, do add interesting variation to the language. The variation that exists in the way a language is spoken is typically the result of the speakers' regional, social, educational, occupational, and language backgrounds.

Variation in pronunciation is common in all languages. However, not everyone finds this variation acceptable. Some people believe there is only one way to pronounce a word—their way. It is interesting that many English speakers, native and non-native alike, are dissatisfied with their own accents.

READING

In the following article, a number of non-native English speakers discuss their feelings about their accents.

Before you begin reading the article, look at the title.

1. What is the meaning of the word "accent" as it is used in the title?
2. Who is the "everyone else" referred to in the title?
3. What feelings do you expect the individuals quoted in the article to have?

For United States immigrants, accent is on sounding like everyone else

by Leu Siew Ying

America is not only a land of immigrants but of accents. From a Southern drawl to a Midwestern twang to California Valspeak, accents define the way we think about each other. But for millions of foreign-born Americans, accents also can mean **humiliation,** job problems, and an **ebbing** self-esteem.

An accent may cost a person business, a job, or a promotion. He may be humiliated because people do not understand him or they make him repeat everything several times.

More and more people with accents—and money—**shell out** $65 an hour to a private speech pathologist to get help.

Chicago **speech pathologist** Bernadette Anderson said that despite the recession she has had more work than she can handle in the past year.

"This has been my most profitable year," she said. . . .

In Chicago, the famous "Da Bulls" accent is not necessarily so funny, pathologists say. A 1988 survey . . . showed that a person who spoke in the typical Chicago nasal twang was seen as "impatient" if he held a supervisory position and "immature" if he was a subordinate.

The recent interest in foreign accent modification has been **spurred** by increased competition in the market-place, experts say.

"People must speak clearly so that they avoid costly mistakes, and there is probably some **antagonism** on the part of native Americans who feel that newly arrived immigrants should speak better English," Daniel Dato [president of Bilingual Language Speech and Hearing Association] said.

The accent that everyone wants is the broad, flat **cadence** spoken by broadcasters like Peter Jennings, a native Canadian, and Great Plains residents, speech pathologists say.

Speech therapists who do accent modification are reluctant to reveal who their clients are and how many they have, but with the 1990 Immigration Act, many expect they will have plenty of business coming their way.

The act raises total legal immigration levels from 540,000 in 1989 to 700,000 a year until 1993.

Many of those with foreign accents do not know they have a problem or how serious it is until they start looking for a job or are assigned new duties.

Rita Galarza, who came here from Ecuador more than 20 years ago when she was 17, was not aware of her accent until she was laid off [after] . . . working for 15 years as a filing clerk.

With her nasal accent she could not find another job.

"I had a big problem finding another job. People are discriminating about accent. I think I can do any kind of job if I have no accent," said Galarza, who

went back to school to earn a master's degree. . . .

Galarza, who is still looking for work, has spent eight hours working on her accent with the help of Anderson. "In the past I felt nervous and upset when people don't understand me. Now when they do not understand me, I ask them: 'Do you speak English?'"

Many like Galarza are seeking help to reduce their accent so that they can raise their self-confidence. Others are highly qualified professionals who write excellent English, but their careers are **jeopardized** by their inability to speak the way Americans want to hear.

Duan Pin Chen is a 27-year-old biophysicist who works in the physiology department [of a hospital].

He was one of 100 Chinese students selected from a field of 10,000 to study in the United States seven years ago, but before he took accent modification classes, few Americans knew much about him because no one here could understand a word he said.

"People who don't know me well looked down on me, and I get angry with myself because I didn't speak the language well," said Chen.

Ten months ago, before he started accent reduction classes, colleagues thought Chen was shy and quiet. Now he surprises his co-workers with his jokes and **bubbly** personality.

"He didn't change as a person but he had been unable to communicate," said department head Robert Eisenberg.

Chen is happy that he speaks more fluently now because he can remember how humiliated he felt before he went for accent reduction classes.

"The American public tends to look down upon people who have an accent," he said.

But not everybody feels happy at having to modify his accent so that Americans can understand him better.

Koshy Vaidyan, an Indian-American electrical engineer who has lived in the United States for 20 years, thinks he speaks better English than Americans because he learned British English in his native India.

But Vaidyan was recently forced to take accent modification classes after clients complained to his boss that they could not understand him.

He claims the complaints are political in nature. "If someone wants something from me he can understand what I say," he said. . . .

Chicago Tribune, Oct. 30, 1991

Vocabulary

humiliation: shame, embarrassment
ebbing: decreasing
shell out: pay
speech pathologist: one who treats pronunciation problems or differences.

spurred: encouraged
antagonism: hostility
cadence: rhythm
jeopardized: exposed to harm
bubbly: spirited

VOCABULARY FOCUS

Accents

1. English speakers use a variety of accents. Examine the above article for adjectives and nouns that describe or name some of these accents. List them below.

   _____

   _____

   _____

2. Can anyone in your class, including your teacher, demonstrate these accents?

JOURNAL

Examining Accent

1. What reasons are given in the article for modifying accents?
2. Which, if any, of the reasons do you agree with?
3. How do the people you speak with react to your accent? Has anyone ever reacted negatively to your accent? What did they say or do?
4. How did you react?
5. How did you feel?
6. Have you considered taking an accent-reduction class? Why or why not?

Threads

The pooh-pooh theory suggests that speech developed from early human noises which were expressed at times of fear, pain, surprise, or joy.

*IT WORKS!
Learning Strategy:
Considering Your
Feelings*

LEARNING STRATEGY

Personalizing: Linking viewpoints of members of your contact culture to those of your native culture increases your understanding of members of your contact culture.

TALK IT OVER

1. Can you think of any times it is appropriate to vary your accent? Or should speakers use just one accent in all of their interactions?
2. Just like speakers of English, speakers of your native language also use different accents. How are these different accents viewed in your native culture? Are people who speak the different accents of your native language thought of in different ways?
3. Have you ever varied your accent in your native language? Why?

8.4 THE WORDS WE USE

COMPARING SYNONYMS

Just as the sounds we use identify us as speakers of particular languages and as members of particular cultures, so do our words. English has the largest vocabulary of any modern language. Partially because of this, English speakers have a range of options to choose from when selecting words. Look at the columns of words below. All the words in a set are similar in meaning. They are synonyms.

gab	hot	yucky	crib
talk	pretty	disgusting	house
converse	exquisite	repugnant	dwelling

"That's hot!!" "That's pretty!" "That's exquisite!"

Find a partner and discuss the following questions regarding the chart of synonyms.

1. How do the words within each set differ in meaning?
2. When would you use the words on the top line rather than those on the middle line or bottom line?
3. How does your knowledge of your contact culture help you choose?

CHECKPOINT

Word choice, like pronunciation, is affected by a number of variables. When speakers or writers choose words, they are often aware of the formality or informality of the situation they are speaking in, the individuals they are speaking to, the types of activities they are engaged in, and the self-image they want to present. Our words, like our pronunciation, identify us as belonging to a certain group. The words we use can even influence peoples' opinions of us.

LEARNING STRATEGY

Overcoming Limitations: Increasing your awareness of specialized language can ease your communication in a greater variety of situations and with a greater variety of individuals.

READING

The author of the following article, Mike Royko, introduces us to "educatorese"—the jargon or specialized vocabulary used by some educators (teachers and administrators) to identify themselves as members of this profession.

1. Do you know of any other professions that have a special vocabulary? If so, what professions?
2. What jargon have you heard people in these professions use?
3. Are you able to understand these words when you hear them?

Now: Talk like an educator!

Until now, only professional educators knew how to speak Educatorese, that mysterious language with which they **befuddle** the rest of us.

But now, for the first time, anyone can learn to speak it.

All you need is the new guide: "How to Speak Like an Educator Without Being Educated."

And as a public service, the guide is being printed in its **entirety** below.

In a moment, I'll provide instructions on its use. But first, a word of credit to its creators.

The guide is the work of two rhetoric and speech teachers at Danville (Ill.) Junior College, Barbara Stover and Ilva Walker. They compiled it after years of wading through administrative **circulars.**

They did it for fun, but some of their students have found that the phrases are useful in preparing papers for sociology classes.

The guide is simple to use.

Take one word from each of the five columns. It doesn't matter which word. Take them in any order, or in no order.

For instance, if you take the second word of Column "A"; the fourth word from Column "B"; the sixth word from Column "C"; and the eighth and tenth words from the last two columns, you will have:

Flexible ontological productivity implement control group and experimental group.

That doesn't make sense, does it? But now add a few connecting words, and we have:

"Flexible and ontological productivity will implement the control group and experimental group."

That still doesn't make any sense. But it sounds like it does. Which means it is perfect Educatorese.

You can do it with any combination of the words. As an example, use the first five digits of my office phone: 321-21.

This works out to:

Adaptable reciprocal nuclei terminate total modular exchange.

Add a few little words and you have a splendid sentence, worthy of at least an assistant **superintendent:**

"Adaptable and reciprocal nuclei will terminate in total modular exchange." And you can quote me on that.

Go to it. With this guide you say things like:

"The interdisciplinary or supportive input will encapsulate vertical team structure."

Or "Optimal ethnic accountability should facilitate post-secondary education enrichment."

Try it yourself. Once you get the hang of it—who knows?—you might wind up with **Superintendent Redmond**'s job.

Vocabulary

befuddle: confuse
entirety: wholeness, fullness
circulars: newsletters
superintendent: a high-ranking school administrator

Superintendent Redmond: superintendent of the Chicago Public Schools in 1973

How to Speak Like an Educator Without Being Educated

A	B	C
comprehensive	cognitive	nuclei
flexible	reciprocal	interaction
adaptable	stylistic	focus
culturally	ontological	balance
perceptual	prime	chain of command
evaluative	supportive	productivity
innovative	workable	conformance
interdisciplinary	resultant	panacea
conceptual	behavioral	rationale
ideological	judgemental	input
optimal	ethnic	throughput
minimal	attitudinal	accountability
categorically	multicultural	feedback
unequivocally	encounter	objective
intrapersonal	counterproductive	resources
interpersonal	generative	perspective
	cognate	curricula
		priorities
		diversity
		environment
		overview
		strategies
		posture
		methodologies
		introversion
		posits
		concept
		Gestalt

D	E
indicates	total modular exchange
terminate	in-depth discussion
geared	multipurpose framework and goals
compile	serial communication
articulate	serial transmission of applicable cable tools
verbalize	and instrumentation
facilitate	post-secondary education enrichment
implement	changing needs of society
incur	motivational serial communications
sensitize	high potential for assessing failure
sythesize	control group and experimental group
integrate	student-faculty relationships
fragment	identifiable decision-making process
maximize	sophisticated resource systems analyses
minimize	vertical team structure
energize	translation in depth
individualize	classroom context
encapsulate	individual horizons
orientate	

From *Sez Who? Sez Me* by Mike Royko

TALK IT OVER

1. Do you understand all of the words listed in this article? If not, how would you figure out the meanings of the words you do not understand?
2. In a dictionary or thesaurus, look up a few of the words listed in the article that you do not understand. Write down the meanings and synonyms you find.
3. Why would someone choose to use the words listed rather than synonyms that would probably be understood more easily by more people?
4. Follow Royko's suggestion and "take one word from each of the five columns." Then, "add a few little words." What do you think of your sentence?
5. Do you agree with Royko that the purpose of speakers of "Educatorese" is to "befuddle the rest of us"?
6. Do you think that this is the only purpose of jargon? What other function or purpose do you see for language that is used mainly by a specific group of people?

Managing Your Learning: Separating large tasks into steps makes them manageable.

Identifying Jargon

Like the educators Royko discusses, many groups have language that is unique to their interests. For example, bankers talk about "deposits," "debits," "wire transfers," and "amortization." Baseball players "steal bases," "slide home," "hit for the cycle," and "fly out." These are all examples of jargon. As your teacher plays the tape, listen to the following play-by-play of a football game to hear jargon in an authentic form. Then do the following activity to identify different kinds of jargon.

1. Look through a newspaper or magazine for an article containing jargon. (*HINT:* Look in the sports, business, fashion, movies, and real estate sections.)
2. Underline all the words that you think are jargon.
3. On a sheet of paper, copy the underlined words into a list.
4. Make five copies of your list and pass them out to five of your classmates.
5. When your classmates receive your list, each one should write his or her name under it.
6. Next to their names, they should write the subject they believe the listed words are related to. (For example, if your list included <u>bases</u>, <u>stealing</u>, <u>sliding home</u>, and <u>hit for the cycle</u>, your classmates would write "baseball" as the related subject.)
7. When your five classmates have identified the topic the jargon is related to, ask them to return your list to you.
8. Compare your classmates' responses. How many of them chose the appropriate subject for your list of words?
9. What do the results tell you about jargon?

Teenspeak

Individuals interested in particular occupations, hobbies, and areas of study are not the only ones who use specialized vocabulary. Different age groups also use unique vocabulary—sometimes referred to as slang.

Read the following article from the *Chicago Sun Times* about the language of teenagers in the United States.

Ad firm tries to crack the code of teenspeak

You say you can't understand your kids?

There's a reason.

They don't speak English, or at least what most of us might call English.

And you probably never will understand it.

The **vernacular** of teenspeak, that language of "gnarly" and "stylin," and "yo" is ever-changing.

But at Chicago's Leo Burnett ad agency, despite all odds, they make it their business to keep up as best they can.

"It's hard," said Jana O'Brien, a Burnett vice president and director of group research, which keeps track of how kids speak. But essential. The improper use of an outdated word in a teen-oriented ad and, well, in the words of a typical New York kid, would simply be "illin'."

(That's something disliked.)

"Kids will quickly reject a message that uses a wrong word," she said.

Burnett regularly surveys teens in Chicago, New York, and L.A., asking them the latest in what's being said. Its most recent survey, taken this summer, reveals hundreds of words in a language that is largely driven by rap music.

"It's a giant **lexicon** being piped across the country," O'Brien said of rap.

The survey is taken every six months because language changes so quickly, though many of the changes are simple variations on existing words.

"Chill," meaning to relax, will evolve to "chillin'" or "chill out" or "take a chill pill."

Researchers have found that, typically, older teens will create the word. It will then filter down to the younger kids. One word that has stayed on the Burnett list for the last few years is "awesome," but it can only be used now to connect with kindergarteners or first-graders, O'Brien said. "You couldn't use 'awesome' with a 16-year-old," she said.

Some words are fairly clear. A positive thing is "excellent" or "mint" in New York and "neato canito" among Californians. Some slang may be familiar. "Groovy" and "happening" are making a comeback. When leaving one place for another, some people say "I'm Outty five thousand"—referring to Audi 5000, the car.

Other times, teenspeak is simply **unfathomable.** Someone who is strange in Chicago might be called a "gym shoe," or if a local teen sees something he likes, he'll describe it as "What up, do'" (pronounced "dough").

Movies and television also play a role. A weird person in Los Angeles is called a "McFly," apparently after a nerdish character of the same name in the "Back to the Future" movies. "Don't have a cow"—meaning to calm down—is a term used by the cartoon character Bart Simpson in the TV show "The Simpsons" and favored among some Chicagoans.

Words can mean different things in different places: "stupid" in New York means something disliked, but in Chicago, "stupid" means something good.

Loyola University Professor Allen Frantzen, who teaches a class on the history of English, said slang is mostly used by people who feel powerless.

"Kids like it because it means they have a code that others can't **crack.** It says to adults, 'You are not on the inside,'" Frantzen said.

Slang has been around for generations, Frantzen said. "Boom," "crank," and "rump" were considered slang in the late 18th and early 19th centuries.

DePaul University English Professor Craig Sirles says the use of slang should not be considered a sign of illiteracy or a lack of education: It's a kind of "wordplay" and indicates "creativity." Sirles calls slang a kind of "personal punctuation."

Sydney Ward, a teacher at Westinghouse Vocational, 3301 W. Franklin, has heard kids use slang throughout his 23 years as an educator.

He tries to de-emphasize it in his classes "so they can be understood when they get out into the real world."

But Ward said he understands why it's so popular.

"It helps them identify with their peer group," he said. "Everyone wants to belong."

So the next time you're wondering just what's being said, "Spaz down" (relax).

They might even think you're a "stony individual," or a really great person.

Vocabulary

vernacular: informal style of language
lexicon: vocabulary
unfathomable: not understandable
crack: figure out

SAY WHA???			
	Chicago	L.A.	N.Y.
Athletes	ballheads	jocks	ballers
Something good	cold	sly	diesel
	dudical	hype	wacked
	strap	fresh	on it
Weird person	gym shoe	jack	skeezer
	outcast	snapper	guff
Hello	hey bum	what'poppin'	you guys bitchen?
	yello	what up G?	what's your age?
Relax	maxin	hangin	cool off
Great person	tripped out	down	fat
	chillin	whipped	bold
Something disliked	spam	to the curve	butt
	rips	booty	nad
Leave	We're casper	bust a move	bolt
	bone out	let's dump	are we away?

Note: Some terms may be used in more than one city.

Andrew Herrmann, *Chicago Sun Times,* Aug. 14, 1992

TALK IT OVER

1. Examine the chart titled "Say Wha???" Which of these words have you heard before? Do you use any of these words?
2. According to the article, why do teens use teenspeak?
3. How do the reasons for using slang compare to those for using jargon? How is slang similar to and different from jargon?

Threads

In one high school in the 70s, students used the expression "snow job" to refer to an assignment done with little preparation or effort.

LEARNING STRATEGY

Remembering New Material: Associating English with your native language increases your understanding of how language is used.

SHARE YOUR EXPERIENCE

In your native country, do different age groups use different words? If so, write down some of the words that young people would use. Then, translate them into English. Are jargon and slang used in your native language in the same way they are used in your contact culture?

8.5 REFLECTING ON WHAT YOU HAVE LEARNED

JOURNAL

Reviewing Your Journey

At the beginning of this chapter, you were asked to consider what it means to be good with language. With the knowledge you have gained through the activities you completed in this chapter, how would you now answer this question? What does it mean to be good with language?

THE JOURNEY CONTINUES

In the following chapter, you will continue your investigation of the relationship between language and culture. Through the activities in Chapter Nine, you will discover what else is involved in "being good with language." As always, we hope your journey is **fresh, good,** and **beneficial.**

The Culture of Language

A different language is a different vision of life.

–Federico Fellini

An aunt of mine kept a hat by her front door, and whenever the doorbell rang, she would put it on. If it was someone she wished to see, she would remark how lucky it was that she had just come in. If it was someone she wanted to avoid, she would say how sorry she was, but she was just going out.

–Jean Pearce in *The Times,* as quoted in *Reader's Digest,* August 1993.

Your understanding of a culture increases with your understanding of its language. As the activities in Chapter 8 illustrated, while you are learning a new language, you need to learn more than the sounds and words of the language. You also need to learn how to adjust your use of these sounds and words so they are appropriate to the background setting they are used in, the people they are used with, and the purpose they are used for.

Threads

Who becomes pregnant without conceiving? Who becomes fat without eating? Answer: Clouds

Babylonian riddle

CONSIDER THIS

What helps a language learner learn how to use the language appropriately? Why is a knowledge of appropriateness important?

_____

_____

_____

_____

_____

A cultural journey is also a language journey. As you learn more about the language of a culture and about how the culture's members use the language, you learn more about the culture. Language is one of the primary voices of culture. Language transmits information that maintains the culture. Language also transmits information that reveals cultural rules and values.

As you continue in Chapter 9 the examination of the relationship between language and culture begun in Chapter 8, your focus shifts from culture as an influence on language use to language use as a reflector of culture. You can learn much about a culture through its language and through its members' language use.

In every culture, there are specific ways to get someone's attention, introduce someone, or refer to someone. The words we use to perform these functions are address forms. Like accent and vocabulary choices, our address form choices are influenced by cultural rules and values.

In the following journal entry, Yoko, an ESL student, questions address form use with her teachers.

Dear Sue:

I don't understand my different teachers. In this class, I call you Sue. That's what you told us to do. I hear some students in my history class call our teacher Mr. Welch. I do, too. I don't know his first name. If I did I don't know if I would use it. I don't hear anyone else do it and he never told us to. My accounting teacher told us to call him Dr. Lawler. I do. He is an old man—older than my other teachers. Does this mean my other teachers aren't doctors? When I walk down the hall I hear different names used for different teachers. Sometimes I hear different names used for the same teacher. What is the right way to call my teachers?

– Yoko

Threads

In Nigeria, a polite greeting consists of a series of questions about the health of family, friends, and fellow workers.

The Curious Book

123

WRITE ABOUT IT

Based on your understanding of your contact culture, what advice do you think Yoko's teacher, Sue, gave her about how to address her teachers? Work with a partner and write Sue's response to Yoko in the form of a letter. Begin your response "Dear Yoko" and sign it "Sue."

LEARNING STRATEGY

Personalizing: By sharing your native cultures, you and your classmates can recognize similarities among your cultures.

CONTRIBUTE YOUR IDEAS

Exchange letters with another set of partners and discuss the following questions:

1. How does the advice in your letters compare?
2. What do you think of the advice to Yoko? Do you follow it when you address your teachers?
3. How do the rules for addressing teachers in your contact culture compare to the rules in your native culture?
4. Which rules are more comfortable for you—the contact culture system or your native system?

One Person, Many Roles

Below is a list of address forms that various individuals may use when addressing Bill Rogers, the president of a construction company in your contact culture. Based on your understanding of your contact culture, which address form or forms do you think each addressor would use? Draw lines between the columns to match each address form with its addressor.

Threads

Abraham Lincoln was often called "Old Abe." General Zachary Taylor, the 12th President, was called "Old Rough and Ready" and "Old Buena Vista."

ADDRESSOR	ADDRESS FORM
His wife	Sir
His daughter	Mr. Rogers
His vice-president	Bill
A construction worker	Dad
His barber	Mr. Bill
His grandmother	Honey
The president of another construction company	President Rogers
	Billy
You	

TALK IT OVER

1. How easy or difficult was it for you to match the address forms with the addressors? Why?
2. What reasons led you to your choices?
3. Can all of the address forms listed be used to address Bill Rogers? Are they equally appropriate? Or are some more appropriate than others?
4. What cultural rules do members of your contact culture follow when making address form choices?
5. What cultural values lead members of your contact culture to make these address form choices?

CULTURE CONNECTION

In Japan, address form usage is also influenced by cultural values. Japanese speakers consider factors like group membership, social position, age, and gender when making address form choices.

How does this system compare to the address form system in your contact culture?

What Form Would You Use?

How do you decide how to address people? How would you address each of the people pictured below? Look at the photographs and read the descriptions. Then, in the space under each picture, write the form you would use if addressing that person.

Betty Tucker
married
D.D.S.
42 years old
your dentist

_____

address form

Lawrence Sims
married
Ph.D.
28 years old
your college instructor

_____

address form

Ling Wang
widow
74 years old
your friend's grandmother

_____

address form

CONTRIBUTE YOUR IDEAS

1. Discuss with two or three classmates your use of address forms for the people pictured on page 125.
2. Discuss whether and how your native cultures influence your decisions.
3. What do you learn about your classmates' cultures from their use of address forms?
4. Do your cultures have similar rules for using address forms?

OBSERVATION TASK

IT WORKS!
Learning Strategy:
Drawing
Conclusions

Observing Address Form Usage

As you walk around on-campus or off-campus, listen to the address forms individuals use. Compile a list of the forms you hear. Following the BEHAVIOR model, also take note of the other observable ingredients—background, individuals, activities, and order—of the cultural behavior of address form usage.

CONTRIBUTE YOUR IDEAS

What rules for the use of address forms can you identify? With your classmates, discuss how the background or setting, the activities engaged in, and the participants in the activities influenced the address form usage. List your rules on the blackboard and in the space below.

CONTACT CULTURE RULES FOR ADDRESS FORM USAGE

TALK IT OVER

1. While gathering data on address forms, did you notice that anyone used an address form in a way you thought was inappropriate? In other words, did you hear anyone violate what you believe to be a rule of address form usage?
2. What message can the violation of an address form rule convey?

OBSERVATION TASK

Interviewing About Address Form Usage

A. Reduce the list of address forms on the blackboard to just those forms that differ from one another. Make a copy of this list for yourself.

B. Find an informant in your contact culture to interview.

C. Show your informant the list of address forms and ask in what situations he or she would use each of the forms. Which forms are more formal, and which are less formal? Are some forms used only with people in certain occupations, in certain social positions, of certain ages, or of a certain gender?

IT WORKS!
Learning Strategy:
Interviewing
Members of Your
Contact Culture

JOURNAL

Comparing Address Form Usage

How do the opinions expressed by your informant compare to your conclusions about address form usage in your contact culture? In what ways are address form usage in your contact culture and in your native culture similar and in which ways do they differ?

9.2 LANGUAGE AND GENDER

As we saw in Chapter 7, one of the organizing structures of a society is gender. In most of the world's cultures, men and women traditionally have specific roles and responsibilities and behave in culturally influenced ways. In U.S. culture, social differences between men and women have revealed themselves in the different ways the genders communicate in their conversational styles.

LISTENING

It is difficult to understand the differences in male and female language just by reading about them. Your teacher will play a tape of two students leaving messages on their professor's answering machine. As you listen to the recording, think about how the man's use of language is different from the woman's.

READING

The following article by Deborah Tannen, a sociolinguist, explores some of the differences in the way men and women use language.

1. Look at the title of the article. What is the meaning of the term "communication gap" in the title of this article?
2. Based on the title, what do you expect the article to discuss?

LEARNING STRATEGY

Overcoming Limitations: Learn more about the reasons underlying language behavior by reading relevant research.

How to close the communication gap between men and women

Although it seems that men and women grow up in the same world, how they use language—in different ways and for different purposes—makes it seem that indeed the two sexes are talking at **cross-purposes.** For women, talk is the glue that holds relationships together; it creates connections between people and a sense of community. For men, activities hold relationships together; talk is used to negotiate their position in a group and preserve independence. With these divergent concerns, women and men typically talk differently when they are trying to achieve the same end. And they often walk away from a conversation having "heard" very different interactions.

. . . Women and men have characteristically different conversational styles. Although there are ethnic, regional, and individual differences in conversation, a vast number of people . . . feel that gender differences account for their behavior and that of their partners, friends and colleagues.

. . . Research by psychologists, sociologists and anthropologists shows that one of the most striking differences between girls' and boys' styles is how they ask—or direct—others to do what they want. At all ages, girls are more likely to phrase their preferences as suggestions, appearing to give others options in deciding what to do. For example, anthropologist Marjorie Harness Goodwin . . . observed girls . . . [making] suggestions like, "Let's go get more bottles," or "Let's wash them because they might have germs in them." They gave reasons for their suggestions, and the reasons involved the good of the group. Goodwin found that boys at play tended to give each other commands like, "Don't come in here where I am!"

. . . Women and men bring these habits and expectations, formed during childhood play, into adulthood. At work, for example, many women are intensely uncomfortable with their bosses who give **bald** commands. One woman said that when her boss gives her instructions, she feels she should salute and say, "Yes, boss!" His directions sounded so **imperious** as to border on the militaristic. Another woman told me that she enjoyed working for a woman who tended to say, for example, "I have a problem. I have to get this report done, but I can't do it myself. What do you think?" Predictably, the employee would offer to write the report.

Though most women understand and appreciate such polite requests, a male employee might find such a request **inscrutable.** If he does perceive that he is being invited to offer to write the report, he might resent being pressured to offer rather than being assigned the task **outright.** People with direct styles of asking for things, including many men, perceive indirect requests as manipulative.

. . . Not perceiving such requests at home may be why some men don't do more work around the house. The husband genuinely may not understand that when the wife says, "The house is really messy, but I don't have time to clean up," she expects him to offer to clean up while she's grocery shopping. A more direct request may be more likely to get the desired result.

. . . Another way that women's and men's styles differ is that most women mix business and personal talk. For example, a woman who directed a counseling center would meet with each staff social worker weekly. When she met with women on the staff, they might spend three-quarters of their time talking about what was going on in their own lives, and a quarter updating the cases and discussing case-related problems. Some of the men on the staff felt that taking time from these business sessions to talk about personal matters was wasted. They believed nonwork discussions about sports or politics, for example, should not be raised during conference hours. They might talk about these things at the coffee machine or before a meeting actually starts, but not during it.

But the women felt that the personal talk established the comfortable relationship between them that provided the basis for working together; it made it possible for them to conduct their business successfully and efficiently.

. . . [W]omen tend to talk more than men at home. [A] man [often] comes home at the end of the day to a woman who will tell him everything that happened to her during the day—if she was home, what the children did and said, where she went and whom she met, who called to tell what news. If she was at work, she will tell him about the people at work, what this or that colleague said, what happened at the meeting, what she said and how it was received. Then she turns to him and asks, "How was your day?"

And he replies: "Okay."

Hurt, she presses, "Didn't anything happen at work?" "Nope," he answers, honestly. "It was just a day like any other." Or he might say, "I had a rotten day; I just want to relax." "What happened?" she encourages, eager to hear his woes. "Oh, nothing special. It was just a rough day, that's all. The usual."

She feels there is something terribly lacking in their relationship, and in him. He's deficient because he isn't in touch with his feelings, doesn't share, doesn't tell her anything. The relationship is deficient because they aren't as close as they should be. When women are asked the reason for their dissatisfaction with marriage, or for their divorces, they say "lack of communication" more often than anything else. I think they are usually referring to this sort of communication—an unstructured give-and-take about daily events, fleeting impressions and feelings that for most women is the essence of intimacy. When the man who is party to the same relationship doesn't mention communication as a problem, he is probably using a different definition of communication: He feels their communication is fine because when they have a major decision to make, they sit down and discuss it. His definition of intimacy is spending time and doing things together.

. . . [T]he most important thing . . . is understanding the differences between women's and men's styles. . . . Our sense of the "right" way to talk, like the right way to behave, is **inextricable** from our sense of being a good person. . . . [C]onversational styles are simply different ways of being polite.

Deborah Tannen , "How to Close the Communication Gap Between Men and Women," McCall's, May 1991 from You Just Don't Understand: Women and Men in Conversation, *William Morrow & Co., 1990*

Vocabulary
cross-purposes: for different reasons
bald: direct, forceful
imperious: authoritative
inscrutable: incomprehensible
outright: directly
inextricable: inseparable

LEARNING STRATEGY

Forming Concepts: Using charts helps you understand abstract concepts.

CONTRIBUTE YOUR IDEAS

With a partner, review Tannen's article and list characteristics of male and female conversational styles in the chart below.

FEMALE	MALE

130

LEARNING STRATEGY

Remembering New Material: Applying the material you read helps store it in your memory.

ASK YOURSELF

Test your understanding of Tannen's article. Read the following survey and think about whether each statement more closely reflects male or female conversational style. If you believe the statement is an example of male language, circle M; if you believe it is an example of female language, circle F.

"The weather is lovely."	M	F
"I'm going to get off at the next exit and look for a place to eat."	M	F
"You've been hungry for a long time, haven't you?"	M	F
"I think I would kind of like to rest for a while."	M	F
"Yeah."	M	F
"Are you sure this is the right exit?"	M	F
"Sure, I always know where I'm going."	M	F

LEARNING STRATEGY

Testing Hypotheses: Interviewing members of your contact culture helps you compare your thoughts about language and gender with theirs.

OBSERVATION TASK

Interviewing About Gender and Language

Tannen believes that if men and women were aware of gender differences in conversational style, they would have fewer miscommunications.

How aware of gender differences in language use do you believe members of your contact culture are?

Find at least two informants and conduct the following survey with one informant at a time. Read these instructions to your informant:

"I am interested in your reaction to the following utterances. I am going to read you a few sentences. For each statement I read, please tell me whether you believe it was originally said by a man or a woman."

Now, read the sentences to your informants. As your informants respond, circle M or F accordingly. After you complete the survey, indicate the gender of your informants in the blanks below the chart.

	1st Informant		2nd Informant	
"The weather is lovely."	M	F	M	F
"I'm going to get off at the next exit and look for a place to eat."	M	F	M	F
"You've been hungry for a long time, haven't you?"	M	F	M	F
"I think I would kind of like to rest for a while."	M	F	M	F
"Yeah."	M	F	M	F
"Are you sure this is the right exit?"	M	F	M	F
"Sure, I always know where I'm going."	M	F	M	F

Gender of Informant   #1. _____   #2. _____

LEARNING STRATEGY

Managing Your Learning: Organizing your informants' responses allows you to observe a pattern in their viewpoints.

CONTRIBUTE YOUR IDEAS

After you and your classmates have completed the survey, bring the results to class. On the blackboard, tally the responses to each statement.

UTTERANCE	female informants		male informants		female students		male students	
	M	F	M	F	M	F	M	F
#1								
#2								
#3								
#4								
#5								
#6								
#7								

TALK IT OVER

Look for a pattern in the responses by discussing the following questions:

1. For each of the utterances, did a majority of the informants agree on the gender of the original speaker?
2. How do the informants' responses compare to the responses of the members of your class?
3. Does there seem to be an awareness, both in your class and among those interviewed, that men and women use language differently?
4. Do men and women seem equally aware of gender differences in language? If not, who seems more aware of these differences?

CULTURAL CONNECTION

Within the Malagasy culture of Madagascar, women's speech is direct. They say exactly what they mean when they express their thoughts and feelings. Women use their direct language to express anger, negotiate at the market, and reprimand children. In contrast, men's language is indirect. By not directly expressing their thoughts and feelings, Malagasy men appear to not command or accuse. They also avoid confrontations. In the Malagasy culture, both men and their language style are more highly valued than women and their language style. How does language use between the genders in Malagasy culture compare to language use as described by Tanner?

LEARNING STRATEGY

Managing Your Learning: Comparing the way children in your native culture and contact culture are raised helps you identify cultural similarities and differences.

Threads

In the past in Morocco, a man could divorce his wife at any time in any place just by repeating three times: "I divorce thee."

The Curious Book

SHARE YOUR EXPERIENCE

1. Do gender differences exist in the use of your native language?
2. What are some of the characteristics of each style?
3. Is one conversational style more highly valued?
4. Do gender differences in language use in your native culture more closely compare to gender differences in your contact culture or in Malagasy culture?

TALK IT OVER

What similarities and differences in male and female conversational style do you find across cultures?

LEARNING STRATEGY

Understanding and Using Emotions: Language and pictures provide channels for exposing your viewpoints.

JOURNAL

Reviewing Your Journey

With the knowledge you have gained through your activities, compose a one-sentence statement that reflects your view of what it means to be "good with language." Be sure to review your response to this question at the end of Chapter 8. If you like, express your view as a metaphor or accompany it with a drawing.

THE JOURNEY CONTINUES

Your exploration of the forms and functions of language has shown you that language, while shared by members of a culture, also varies among members. People use language to create a common body of cultural knowledge. People also use language to mark themselves as individuals.

Your journey to cultural understanding brings you next to an exploration of the ways media spreads information within a culture. Language—whether it be the language of the individual or the institution—is the channel of culture.

The Channels of Culture

No one is poor except he who lacks knowledge...

A person who has knowledge has everything.
A person who lacks knowledge, what has he?

Once a person acquires knowledge, what does he lack?
If a person does not acquire knowledge, what does he possess?

–Babylonian Talmud

CONSIDER THIS

Newspapers, magazines, television, and advertising are four ways cultural information is spread to and shared by members of a culture. Look at the headlines, TV program summaries, and advertisements above. Also, listen to the taped conversation your teacher will play for you. Based on what you see and hear, what is the role of the media in a culture?

_____

_____

_____

_____

_____

Culture, by definition, informs. For a culture to be maintained in the current generation and to be transferred to following generations, individual members must be informed of cultural knowledge. Members of a culture are kept informed through a variety of cultural media. In this chapter, we examine the roles of newspapers, magazines, television, and advertising in keeping those members informed of the people and events that affect their lives.

In 1990, 1,611 daily newspapers were published in the United States—1,084 afternoon publications and 559 morning papers. The number of newspapers has been slowly declining for decades, in part because of radio and television, but also because, in the fight for readers and advertising, competing papers have battled until a single winner emerged. . . . Daily **circulation** has hovered around 60 million for 15 years or so, with a total of 62,324,156 in 1990. The average paper sells under 50,000 copies a day, and 156 have a daily circulation of more than 100,000. However, the 26 largest newspaper chains account for more than 80% of total daily circulation, reflecting a trend that started in the 1970s.

—Universal World Almanac

Threads

"Were it left to me to decide whether we should have a government without newspapers, or newspapers without government, I should not hesitate for a moment to prefer the latter."

Thomas Jefferson (1787)

circulation: number of copies sold

TALK IT OVER

1. Based on these circulation figures, newspapers reach at least one-quarter of the United States population each day. What is the role of a newspaper in a culture? What cultural functions do newspapers fulfill?
2. What effect does such widespread circulation of newspapers have on a culture?

LEARNING STRATEGY

Forming Concepts: Using key words and phrases guides your understanding of a text.

Tables of Contents

CONTRIBUTE YOUR IDEAS

Bring a newspaper published in your community to class. Find the table of contents. With two or three of your classmates who have brought in other newspapers, combine your tables of contents, making a list of all the sections in your newspapers.

Write the names of the sections common to all the newspapers in the space in the chart on the next page.

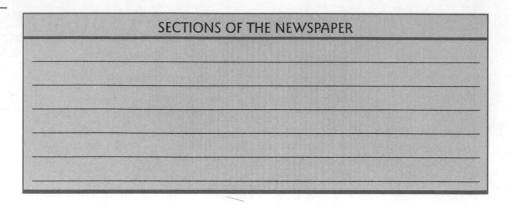

SECTIONS OF THE NEWSPAPER

1. Based on the titles of these sections, what do you expect their contents to be?
2. Which sections do you believe the newspapers' editors feel are most important?
3. How do you decide? Do you look at the size of the section, its location in the paper, the number of articles it contains, or some other evidence?
4. Order the sections you have listed above by their importance from most important to least important. First, order them as you believe the newspapers view them. Second, order them as you believe they reflect the values of your contact culture.
5. How does your list compare to your classmates' lists? What values did your classmates decide the newspaper sections reflect?

SHARE YOUR EXPERIENCE

1. If possible, bring to class a newspaper that is popular in your native culture. Explain to your classmates how the contents of this newspaper compare to those of the newspapers in your contact culture. Are the contents similar or different? In what ways?
2. Do the differences reflect different cultural values in your native and contact cultures?

Tabloids

Tabloids provide another channel for printed news. Published weekly, tabloids are often displayed for sale in the check-out line at grocery stores. Listed below are the names of some tabloids and some headlines of articles they have published.

National Enquirer
"Oprah's Show is Haunted"
"Dressed to Drill: The Toughest Sergeant in this Man's Army is a Lady"
"Would You Give Up Sex for $1 Million?"
"Cheers' Star's Wife Loses Baby After Suicide Bid"
"Overweight? You Can <u>Still</u> Be Fit"

National Examiner
"Why Marilyn Had to Die: Secret FBI Files Reveal She Knew Too Much"
"Miracle Surgery Gives 4-legged Baby a Normal, Healthy Life: Touching Before-and-After Photos"

Globe
"The Way We Were: Exclusive Photos of the First Moment Bill and Hillary Met"
"Hollywood's Newest Secret to Stay Young: Stars Eat Crushed Pearls"
"Oprah's Wedding Snub Lands Her Mom in Hospital"
"Revealed! Princess Di was an Abused Child"

Sun
"Fishermen Pull Living Baby Out of Shark's Belly: He's Alive and Kicking"
"I'm Lonely for Love—Says Man Who Smells Like a Skunk"
"Dad and 2 Sons Forced to Rob Homes to Pay Medical Bills"
"What Your Pet Reveals About You: The Animal You Prefer Reveals Your Personality"
"Electric Shock Cures Woman's Migraines"

IT WORKS!
Learning Strategy:
Discussing Your
Opinions

CONTRIBUTE YOUR IDEAS

1. Based on these headlines, how do the articles in tabloids differ from those in daily newspapers?
2. Why would people find tabloids interesting to read?
3. Do you think that the subject matter of tabloids also reflects cultural values and beliefs? If so, what are these values and beliefs?
4. Are tabloids popular in your native country? If so, are they popular for the same or different reasons they are popular in your contact culture?
5. Look again at the article titles and headlines that have appeared in tabloids. Would these headlines and titles attract readers in your native country? If not, what kinds of headlines would be of interest in your native country?

WRITE ABOUT IT

If there is another student in your class from your native country, work together to create a tabloid headline that reflects interests, values, or beliefs of your native culture. If you are the only representative of your native culture in your class, you may work alone to create a headline.

CONTRIBUTE YOUR IDEAS

Share your headline with your classmates and explain why it would be of interest to members of your culture.

Comics

One of the most widely read sections of the newspaper is the comic section. Most newspapers include at least 20 comic strips each day.

TALK IT OVER

1. What do you believe is the purpose of comic strips?
2. Do you read comic strips? If so, which ones?
3. What is the content of these strips? What ideas or topics do they cover?

READING

While comic strips historically have offered humorous views of life, in recent years some have taken a more serious tone. The article that follows explores some of the reasons for this shift in focus.

Comic strips get serious

by Staci D. Kramer

Last week, 17-year-old Lawrence Poirier told his best friend, Michael Patterson, that he was gay. Similar scenes take place regularly these days—but not in Lawrence's neighborhood. (1)

Lawrence lives on more than 1,400 comics pages nationwide in Lynn Johnston's "For Better or for Worse." . . . (2)

In "For Better or for Worse" he lives near Elly and John Patterson and their three children, Michael, Lizzie, and April. (3)

Lawrence and his creator have known for several years that he's gay; in fact, he tells Michael he is in love with another young man. He blurted out the truth after Michael repeated a remark made by Lawrence's mother about future grandchildren. (4)

Lawrence isn't the first gay character in a comic strip. That distinction goes to Andy, the lawyer in "Doonesbury" who came out in 1977 while dating Joanie Caucus. Thirteen years later, readers learned that Andy had AIDS in a storyline laced with pathos and absurdity and, in 1991, watched him die. (5)

But Lawrence is part of a trend that allows comic-strip children and teenagers to deal with some of the more serious issues affecting their real-life counterparts. (6)

Johnston, the strip's Canadian author, has been on the cutting edge with stories about shoplifting, the death of an elderly neighbor, child abuse, preteen smoking, and teenage drinking. She introduced an Asian family and a teacher in a wheelchair. (7)

Once the "gay" storyline concludes . . . , she does not intend to revisit the issue. "I wanted Lawrence to be known as a gay individual, but that would not be the important part of his life," she explained. . . . (8)

She expected some of the outrage that a few editors have expressed. [In response to the storyline,] seven papers had canceled the strip and 13 more had either stopped running it or asked for substitute material. (9)

"For all the people who say this shouldn't be in the comics, please write all of the television stations who put garbage on," Johnston said. "This is a banana peel compared to the hordes of pollution that's on television." . . . (10)

Cartoonist Greg Evans takes a similar approach in his strip "Luann." In 1991, he shocked readers with a story about 13-year-old Luann starting her period. Some were outraged, but many, especially teens, wrote in to thank Evans for dealing with an important topic in a sensitive, yet humorous way. (11)

Last fall, Evans carefully stepped into another controversy when Luann's older brother Brad took along a condom on a first date. It fell out of his wallet as he paid for movie tickets, forcing Brad to explain to his date that he respected her too much to want to need the condom, but enough to make sure he had one. (12)

The series ended with a laugh when the condom fell out of the wallet again as Brad tried once more to pay for the tickets. (13)

During the same storyline, Brad and his father spent several panels discussing sex. Typically embarassed by the topic, his father finally suggested abstinence as the best option at his son's age. (14)

Bill Amend, the Kansas City-based creator of "Fox Trot," . . . doesn't think his father and son characters are ready for that kind of discussion. (15)

"With my own strip I try to create a reasonably realistic reflection of American culture, and so early on I decided I wasn't going to stick with just an idealized cast of characters. In addition to having a blind character, my characters at times display traits that many readers consider less than ideal." (16)

Denise, the blind teenage girl, is older son Peter's first real girlfriend. Her blindness often plays a role in the strip, but usually the two face the same problems that might happen to any dating teens. Younger son Jason has a black best friend who is just as nerdy as he is. (17)

"I think particularly when you're writing with a younger audience in mind that if you try to convey a particular message in too heavy-handed a way, they'll tune it out," he said. (18)

For instance, Amend could alienate readers by preaching the gospel of homework. But if he shows the consequences of a well-liked character putting off an assignment, the message comes through loud and clear. (19)

Sometimes, being realistic means trying to avoid stereotypes. Amend realized that by making Paige, a teenage girl, bad at math he was sending a negative message to young female readers. (20)

Recently, in an effort to change the stereotype, he showed Paige dissecting a frog and finding out she was good at it. (21)

"I was criticized for being politically incorrect having Paige be dumb at math, then yelled at by animal rights activists for portraying animal dissection as fun," he recalled ruefully. (22)

These cartoonists constantly must balance social relevance with attempts to please a diverse readership. (23)

New York's Ray Billingsley walks a narrow line sometimes as creator of "Curtis," which is one of the few strips starring a black family. . . . Older strips like "Hi and Lois" and "Peanuts" reflect a simpler vision of life, cartoonist Billingsley believes. "The kids' greatest problem is finding bread for their jelly sandwich. For most of us, life is a little harder than that. We're trying to find the bread and the jelly for our sandwich." (24)

–Chicago Tribune, *March 29, 1993*

VOCABULARY FOCUS

Listed below are the definitions of some of the words in the reading. In parentheses next to each definition is the number of the paragraph in which you can find the word. Write the word next to its definition.

compassion (5) _____

ridiculousness (5) _____

current (7) _____ (phrase)

stealing from a store (7) _____

anger (9) _____

great amount (10) _____

menstruation (11) _____

avoidance of sex (14) _____

perfect (16) _____

to make someone feel unfriendly (19) _____

giving advice to do a particular thing (19) _____ (phrase)

results (19) _____

cutting up of an animal (21 and 22) _____

sadly (22) _____

LEARNING STRATEGY

Understanding and Using Emotions: Considering your feelings about the presentation of social issues by various media channels acquaints you with other people's views.

TALK IT OVER

1. What do you think about cartoonists including socially relevant messages in their comic strips? Do you believe comic strips can deal with important topics "in a sensitive, yet humorous way"?
2. Do you agree that cartoonists must "balance social relevance with attempts to please diverse readership"? Are there particular social issues that are not appropriate for cartoonists to address in comic strips?
3. Bill Amend, creator of "Fox Trot" says he was "criticized for being politically incorrect for having Paige be dumb in math." What is meant by "politically incorrect"?

OBSERVATION TASK

Comic Strips in Your Contact Culture
1. Find the comic pages in a newspaper published in your contact culture.
2. Read each of the comic strips.
3. Bill Amend claims he is trying to "create a reasonably realistic reflection of American culture" in his comic strip. What reflections of your contact culture can you identify in the comic strips you read?

Threads

"Winnie Winkle," a famous comic strip begun in 1920 by Martin Branner, was the first to have a career-girl as the main character.

SHARE YOUR EXPERIENCE

Are comic strips a channel of cultural or social information in your native culture?

If you can, bring in one or more comic strips from a newspaper published in your native country. Share them with your classmates. If necessary, translate the language of the strip into English for your classmates. Are these comic strips "a reasonably realistic reflection" of your native culture?

10.2 MAGAZINES

Like newspapers, magazines are a primary source of information to and about a culture. Like newspapers, too, magazines are extremely popular in the United States. In 1989, 11,556 different magazines were published in the United States, according to the Universal World Almanac. Combined circulation in 1990 for the one hundred best-selling magazines in the United States was 261,688,396. Given that the total population of the United States in 1990, according to the census, was 248,709,873, it is clear that magazines occupy a major media position in U.S. culture.

LEARNING STRATEGY

Forming Concepts: Analyzing statistics enables you to identify cultural patterns.

READING

Magazine Circulation

Below is a table that lists the top twelve United States magazines by monthly (or weekly) circulation as of 1990. Examine the table and the accompanying descriptions of their content and intended audience.

TOP 100 U.S. MAGAZINES, BY CIRCULATION, 1990		
RANK	**MAGAZINE**	**CIRCULATION**
1	*Modern Maturity*	22,430,894
2	*NRTA/AARP Bulletin*	22,103,887
3	*Reader's Digest*	16,264,547
4	*TV Guide*	15,604,267
5	*National Geographic Magazine*	10,189,703
6	*Better Homes and Gardens*	8,007,222
7	*Family Circle*	5,431,779
8	*Good Housekeeping*	5,152,521
9	*McCall's*	5,020,127
10	*Ladies' Home Journal*	5,001,739
11	*Woman's Day*	4,802,824
12	*Time*	4,094,935

–Universal World Almanac

Modern Maturity and the *NRTA/AARP Bulletin* are available monthly and only by mail to members of the American Association of Retired People—an organization whose members, still working or retired, are at least 50 years of age.

Reader's Digest, also a monthly, primarily publishes condensed articles and stories from other magazines and books.

TV Guide offers weekly program listings and articles of interest to television viewers.

National Geographic Magazine publishes articles on and prints maps and photographs of places and cultures throughout the world.

Better Homes and Gardens, Family Circle, Good Housekeeping, McCall's, Ladies' Home Journal, and *Woman's Day* are marketed primarily to women with an interest in home care and decorating, childcare, cooking, fashion, and health. These magazines offer articles, recipes, and craft ideas.

Time is a news magazine that presents and analyzes events and people throughout the world but primarily those of interest to members of U.S. culture.

TALK IT OVER

What conclusions about United States culture do these statistics lead you to form?

LEARNING STRATEGY

Testing Hypotheses: Examining a magazine's content verifies your hypotheses.

OBSERVATION TASK

Scanning Magazines

1. Visit a magazine rack at a bookstore, grocery store, or library. Write down the names of ten of the magazines. (Look for titles other than the twelve already discussed.)
2. Based on their titles and on the information and pictures on their covers, write down your predictions about the content and intended audience of each of the magazines.
3. Choose three of the magazines from your list of ten to look at in more detail. How do their actual contents and intended audiences compare to your predictions?
4. Each of these magazines is a medium of information. Each is also a channel of cultural values. What cultural values are addressed by the magazines you looked at?

CONTRIBUTE YOUR IDEAS

Buy one magazine and bring it to class. Show the magazine to your classmates and describe it by answering the following questions:

- What is its title?
- Who is its intended audience?
- What are its contents?
- What cultural values does it address?
- Is this magazine available in your native culture and your native language?
- If so, does it address the same cultural values in your native culture as in your contact culture?
- If not, why do you think it is unavailable? Does the magazine address values that are irrelevant to your native culture?

Television programs are created to appeal to different segments of a culture. Some programs are designed to appeal to a female audience, some to a male audience; some programs are designed for children, some for adults.

CONTRIBUTE YOUR IDEAS

Daily newspapers typically include a schedule of that day's television programming. Find one of these schedules in a newspaper from your contact culture and bring it to class.

With the members of your group, take note of the different stations and the kinds of programs they broadcast. Choose four stations that to you seem to have a specific audience in mind. In the chart below, record the name of each of these stations and the interests viewers of this station and its programs have.

NAME OF STATION	INTERESTS OF VIEWERS

Threads

TVs are present in 98.2% of U.S. households and watched an average of seven hours and one minute per day.

Television Bureau of Advertising, 1991

READING

A View of TV

The following excerpt from *Conscientious Objections: Stirring Up Trouble About Language, Technology, and Education* discusses the role of television in a culture.

. . . "One might say that the main difference between an adult and a child is that the adult knows about certain **facets** of life—its mysteries, its contradictions, its violence, its tragedies—that are not considered suitable for children to know. As children move toward adulthood, we reveal these secrets to them in ways we believe they are prepared to manage. That is why there is such a thing as children's literature.

"But television makes this arrangement impossible. . . . It requires a constant supply of novel and interesting information to hold its audience. This means that all adult secrets—social, sexual, physical and the like—are revealed. Television forces the entire culture to **come out of the closet,** taps every existing **taboo.** . . . As a consequence of all this, childhood innocence is impossible to **sustain.**"

—Neil Postman

Vocabulary
facets: parts, aspects
come out of the closet: reveal the truth
taboo: unmentionable topic
sustain: maintain, hold on to

TALK IT OVER

1. What is your reaction to Postman's view of television? Do you believe that television robs children of their innocence?
2. If so, what behaviors have you observed in children or what have you heard children say that supports your belief?
3. Is Postman's argument also relevant to the role of television in your native culture? Why or why not?

LISTENING

Talk Show Topics

The number of television talk shows has increased over the last few years as viewer interest in world issues, the troubles of celebrities, and the personal problems of average individuals has grown. As your teacher plays the tape, listen to the schedule for one day of television talk show programming. Note the topics of the various programs.

CONTRIBUTE YOUR IDEAS

Do these topics lend support to Postman's views? How?

LEARNING STRATEGY

Managing Your Learning: Focus your analysis by planning to observe specific components.

OBSERVATION TASK

Television Talk Shows

Watch one talk show broadcast in your contact culture. Following the BEHAVIOR Model, take notes on what you see. Describe the background or setting of the talk show, the individuals present, the activities and their order, and the topics of their verbal exchanges. Attempt to determine their hopes and values. And attempt to infer the rules that guide their interaction.

CONTRIBUTE YOUR IDEAS

Share the findings of your talk show observation with a few of your classmates.

1. What are your reactions to the topics discussed on the show you watched?
2. How comfortable were you listening to the discussion of these topics?
3. Did you learn anything new from the discussion?
4. How did the discussion add to your understanding of your contact culture?

JOURNAL

Talk Shows

In your native culture, is there anything like television talk shows? Is there a place where people can talk about and listen to personal problems and social issues? Is it on television or radio talk shows or is there a different outlet for this information? What kinds of topics are appropriate to discuss in public?

Of all the media that reach out to the members of a culture, advertising is perhaps the most dominant. The majority of broadcast advertisements and commercials are for material goods and services that members of the culture have developed an interest in and that, in turn, have come to occupy an important place in their lives. Therefore, the ads that show up on television and radio and in newspapers and magazines reflect values held by various members of the culture.

A Look at Slogans

Most ads contain a slogan—a sentence or phrase that the ad's creators hope will come to be associated with the product and will then remind consumers of its function. Slogans can take different forms. They can explain the product, invite consumers to use the product, or create a picture to help us visualize the benefits of the product.

Below is a list of slogans. Try to match each slogan with the corresponding product. When you finish, compare your answers to those of a classmate and then to those at the bottom of page 150.

SLOGAN	PRODUCT
_____ When you care enough to send the very best	a. Burger King
_____ The good times never lasted longer	b. Hallmark
_____ Have it your way	c. Eveready Energizer
_____ Good to the last drop	d. Nike
_____ Advanced medicine for pain	e. Maxwell House Coffee
_____ Just do it	f. Advil

TALK IT OVER

1. Which of these slogans have you seen or heard before?
2. Which are new to you?
3. How did you decide which slogan to match with which product?
4. What clues do the slogans provide?

150

LEARNING STRATEGY

Remembering New Material: Searching for examples of advertising strategies reinforces and helps you to remember them.

OBSERVATION TASK

Going on a Slogan Hunt

A. Collect at least 10 slogans by looking through magazine or newspaper ads, listening to commercials, or observing billboards. Write down the slogans and the products or services they endorse. Bring your list to class.

B. Divide your class into two teams. Combine your slogans with those collected by the other members of your team. Read aloud one slogan at a time to the other team and see if they can name the product.

NOTE: You may want to set a time limit for each team to answer.

LEARNING STRATEGY

Managing Your Learning: Narrow your task by focusing on specific goals.

ANALYZING SLOGANS

The people who invent advertising slogans use different methods to make their slogans creative and memorable. Some of these methods are listed below with sample slogans.

A. A slogan with the product name embedded in it.

> EXAMPLE: "Hanes makes you feel good all under."
> (Hanes underwear)

_____

_____

B. A slogan that introduces the product function.

> EXAMPLE: "Clean your breath while you clean your teeth."
> (Crest toothpaste)

_____

_____

C. A slogan that describes the product.

> EXAMPLE: "The Chocolate Laxative"
> (Ex-Lax)

_____

_____

Answers to slogans on page 149: b, c, a, e, f, d

D. A slogan that instructs you to buy the product.

> EXAMPLE: "Don't wait to be told—you need Palmolive Gold."
> (Palmolive)

_____

_____

E. A slogan that includes a play on words.

> EXAMPLE: "Where advanced technology has striking results"
> (Ebonite Bowling Balls)

_____

_____

F. A slogan that is directed to your emotions.

> EXAMPLE: "You're in good hands"
> (Allstate Insurance)

_____

_____

G. A slogan that is directed primarily to men.

> EXAMPLE: "The best a man can get"
> (Gillette)

_____

_____

H. A slogan that is directed primarily to women.

> EXAMPLE: "Often a bridesmaid, never a bride"
> (Listerine)

_____

_____

I. A slogan that is directed primarily to children.

> EXAMPLE: "They're gr-r-reat!"
> (Kellogg's Frosted Flakes)

_____

_____

Examine the slogans collected by your classmates. Among these slogans, find
as many examples as you can of each of the methods in the list above. Write the
appropriate slogans on the lines following each method.

TALK IT OVER

Advertising is a way to attract consumers to products and services. When advertisers write slogans, they pay close attention to cultural values and to the specific needs of individuals in the culture.

1. What kinds of needs or interests do the slogans you collected address?
2. What values of your contact culture do these slogans reflect?

SHARE YOUR EXPERIENCE

IT WORKS!
Learning Strategy:
Talking About Your
Native Culture

1. How are advertisements and commercials in your contact culture similar to and different from those in your native culture?
2. Are the products and services advertised in your contact culture available in your native culture?
3. Are they advertised similarly? If not, would some of these products or services not be advertised at all? Why not?

BE A CULTURAL INFORMANT

1. If you can, bring in an ad from a newspaper or magazine published in your native culture. Show it to your classmates and explain its contents.
2. Why does the product or service advertised appeal to members of your native culture?
3. What cultural values do the product and the ad reflect?

CREATE A SLOGAN

Threads

A fertility specialist advertised his business with the sign, "From Here to Paternity."

Mary Jo Hillery (Quoted from "Diversion" in *Reader's Digest*)

A. In a group with one or two other students, think up a product or service that you believe will appeal to individuals living in your contact culture. The product or service may address either a serious or amusing need. Then, create a slogan for this product or service. If you like, you may even create a drawing to represent the product or service.

B. Describe your product or service to your classmates and share your slogan. As you discuss your slogan, answer the following questions:

1. Why would your product or slogan appeal to members of your contact culture?
2. Which cultural values does your product or service address?
3. How have you created your slogan to address these values?

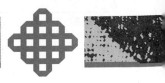

JOURNAL

In these days of increased contact between cultures, we need to think, too, about the increased exchange of cultural media.

What effect does the media of one culture have on the members of another culture?

Consider the following article as you compose your response.

Russians usher in age of U.S. TV

by Laurel Campbell

Moscow—Turn down the sound on the TV, and you might think you never left America.

Chip n' Dale cartoons, the soap opera "Santa Barbara," American movies, and even Head & Shoulders shampoo commercials are all around the dial on Russian TV. Or by **flicking** the remote control—Russians share a lot of bad habits with Americans.

But they don't have as many TV sets. In Russia, there is one TV set for every three persons; in the United States, the ratio is nearly 1-to-1.

"My parents bought their first color TV five years ago," said Julia Isaeva, a 26-year-old Muscovite. . . .

Russians are also getting used to freedoms of speech and art, welcomed or not, on TV and radio and in movies, newspapers and magazines. Beginning in 1986, **glasnost** brought new independence to state-controlled news outlets. . . .

There are hundreds of video rental stores in Moscow, sometimes just small spaces in beauty shops and other businesses.

"Probably 90 percent of the videos are foreign movies," Isaeva said.

"After 70 years of just showing films about the production of steel and oil, people want to see something different."

Like "Terminator." And "Silence of the Lambs." Both American blockbusters were available on videocassette in Moscow just months after they appeared in the United States.

"Five years ago, having a VCR was not common. It's still expensive—like having a fur coat—but not unusual," Isaeva said. . . .

American films are also in Russian movie theaters; "Pretty Woman" was showing in Volgograd late last year.

"Since **perestroika,** there are lots of trashy Russian movies featuring gangsters, violence and sex," said Sergey Vovchenko, a 28-year-old Volgograd resident. . . .

"There's nothing to see these days," said one **usher,** explaining why so few people were waiting for the early-evening, half-price show. A ticket cost 50 rubles—less than 20 cents.

Two years ago, the usher said, "Gone With the Wind" played for a year to sellout showings. . . .

"Duck Tales" and Chip 'n' Dale cartoons are popular on Russian TV. So is a children's puppet show, "Goodnight, Babies," that airs every evening. The star is a pig puppet named Hrusha.

Children's parents, meanwhile, avidly follow a long-running Mexican series translated as "The Rich Also Cry."

Episodes are broadcast in the morning and evening.

Breakfast-time TV fare includes "Morning," a news magazine **clone** of the "Today" show, **anchored** by a two-man, one-woman team. The **slick** show includes international news, weather and sports.

On one day, a clip of Frank Sinatra singing "Mack the Knife" in a recording studio closed out the show while the credits **rolled.**

The most popular Russian TV program, and the most expensive for advertisers, is a Friday night game show called "Land of Miracles." Three players vie for prizes by answering questions in front of a live audience. . . .

Radio choices include Radio 7 Moscow, a Russian-American joint venture that plays American rock. U.S. visitors may not understand the Russian-speaking announcer, but there's no mistaking Elvis doing "Suspicious Minds."

Russians also know **"PROCK-ter & GAM-bell,"** as the announcer says in the TV commercial for Head and Shoulders. When the ad came on the screen during an episode of "The Rich Also Cry," a roomful of girls in St. Petersburg started laughing.

"I'm sorry," one said, "but we're sick and tired of this commercial."

Chicago Tribune

153

Vocabulary

flicking: pressing the buttons

glasnost: a political policy promoting openness

perestroika: a political philosophy promoting democracy

usher: an employee of a movie theater

clone: an exact copy

anchored: hosted

slick: polished, professional

rolled: appeared on the screen, went by

PROCK-ter & GAM-bell: (Procter & Gamble) a U.S. corporation
that manufactures cleaning and health care products.

THE JOURNEY CONTINUES

In this chapter, you have examined the relationship between culture and media such as newspapers, magazines, television, and advertising. You have investigated how the content of these media reflect and perhaps influence cultural values. In Chapter 11, you will take a closer look at cultural values. You may already recognize that values underlie the rules that structure a person's behavior. What you may not recognize is the variety of ways in which values are reflected in a culture.

Cultural Values

11

CHAPTER

*If you have built castles in the air,
your work need not be lost;
that is where they should be.
Now put the foundations under them.*

-Henry David Thoreau

Tell all the Truth but tell it slant—
Success in Circuit lies
Too bright for our infirm Delight
The Truth's superb surprise
As Lightening to the Children eased
With explanation kind
The Truth must dazzle gradually
Or every man be blind—
      -Emily Dickinson

TALK IT OVER

1. What value is Emily Dickinson conveying in the poem?
2. How does she suggest that truth be told?
3. Americans are often accused of being direct in truth-telling, even blunt. Yet, Emily Dickinson is an American poet. Which view of telling the truth—telling it slant, or telling it directly—do you think represents an American cultural value?

Throughout this book, as you have observed and analyzed behaviors, you have often been asked to identify the values associated with these behaviors. As you know, the values that underlie the rules that structure behaviors are not observable. Rather, they must be inferred. The activities in Chapter 10 revealed some of the ways media expresses the values of a culture. The activities in this chapter will reinforce the idea that cultural knowledge goes beyond what you can see to include what you must infer. Knowledge of values is key to the complete understanding of a culture.

CONSIDER THIS

Read the following quote from Marvin Mayers, an anthropologist.

"No community exists without values. Values are whatever an individual within a group considers of importance. In each automatic or consciously made decision some value underlies the choice of one thing over against another."

1. What does the last sentence mean? Give an example of how it may work.
2. Since values are so prevalent, yet unobservable, how can they be determined accurately? Write your response below.

_____

_____

_____

_____

_____

_____

_____

Threads

In the Navajo culture, the concept of collective responsibility, which makes each person in a family responsible for the behavior of each other, is central to maintaining order in the society.

11.1 BEHAVIOR AND CULTURAL VALUES

As you know, cultural behaviors are structured by rules. In the following activities you will be focusing on behaviors that are of great importance in structuring society—those that are structured by the cultural rules of time.

SHARE YOUR EXPERIENCE

IT WORKS!
Learning Strategy:
Focusing on Your
Native Culture

In pairs, discuss the following questions regarding the concept of time in your native cultures.

1. When you are invited to supper at someone's house, what time should you arrive? What does it mean to be too early or too late? How long should you stay?
2. Define punctuality. How important is punctuality in your culture? In which situations is it most important? Least important?
3. How would you describe the pace of life in your country? Do people often hurry? When might they hurry?
4. Where are clocks found in your culture? Are the clocks usually accurate? Does it matter how accurately they are set?
5. In social gatherings, such as a church meeting or a community meeting where someone might be asked to give a speech, is the person given a time limit? If so, how important is it for the person to stick to the time limit? What happens if the person talks for 5, 10, or 15 minutes longer? What happens if the person speaks for the exact time given to him or her?

OBSERVATION TASK

Time Rules

Choose an event in your contact culture to attend, such as a lecture, a musical or theatrical event, a community event, or a religious service. While you are there, gather data related to the following questions as well as to the components of the BEHAVIOR model.

IT WORKS!
Learning Strategy:
Reviewing Your
Observation
Checklist

- Did the event begin at the time stated?
- Did people arrive at the time stated? How many came in later? What reactions did the people already there have toward those who came in later? Were the latecomers noticed?
- Were people wearing watches? Did you notice people looking at their watches? How often and when?
- Did you hear any comments about time as people were leaving or arriving?

SHARE YOUR EXPERIENCE

IT WORKS!
Learning Strategy:
Summarizing Your
Observations

1. Give an oral report of your experience to your class. Using the BEHAVIOR model to structure your presentation will help your classmates picture what it was like to attend the event that you describe.
2. Share your findings regarding the above questions. What do your observations reveal about the cultural value of time held by participants in the event you observed?

LEARNING STRATEGY

Overcoming Limitations: Increase your understanding of your contact culture by listening to your classmates' analyses.

TALK IT OVER

1. What does it mean to people in your contact culture to be "on time" or to be "late"?
2. What patterns of behavior did you observe in regard to time?
3. The English language is filled with phrases about time. Based on the oral reports from your classmates, which of the following phrases best represent the value of time in your contact culture?

Be on time.	*Time heals all wounds.*
Got a minute?	*Better late than never.*
See you later.	*Rome was not built in a day.*
Time is money.	*A stitch in time saves nine.*
Don't waste time.	*I'll be back in a little while.*
Haste makes waste.	*I need to spend some time with you.*
You are just in time.	*Never put off until tomorrow what you*
Patience is a virtue.	*can do today.*

Can you think of any more?

Forming Concepts: Finding similarities in the meanings of proverbs can help you identify cultural values.

SHARE YOUR EXPERIENCES

1. Benjamin Franklin said, "Do not squander time, for that's the stuff life is made of." Would people from your culture agree with his statement? Why or why not?
2. What are some of the proverbial sayings or metaphors that your culture has regarding time?

JOURNAL

The Value of Time
How would you describe the cultural value placed on time in your contact culture? How does this compare to your native culture?

11.2 PROVERBS: CLUES TO CULTURAL VALUES

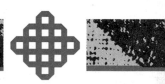

Understanding and Using Emotions: Considering the meaning of proverbs in a culture allows you to understand the feelings of its members.

READING

Below are a few West African proverbs. What inferences can you make about the values of the people who use these proverbs?

Proverbs of West Africa
1. Loss of teeth and marriage spoil a woman's beauty.
2. If you have escaped the jaws of the crocodile while bathing in the river, you'll surely meet a leopard on the way.
3. Stay away from an open toilet, and you'll not be annoyed by the stench.
4. Correct announcements cannot be made by beating only one side of the drum.

5. He who would sweep the hut must not sit on the broom.
6. When the head is off, dreaming will cease.
7. No chicken will fall into the fire a second time.
8. Do not play with the tail of a dog, and you will not be bitten.
9. The foolishness of a man will not become known as quickly as that of a woman.
10. The shoulder (the woman) is not above the head (the man).
11. A talkative bird will not build a nest.

CONTRIBUTE YOUR IDEAS

Write at least three cultural values that you can infer from these proverbs.

1. _____

2. _____

3. _____

When you finish, compare your list with a partner's and discuss which specific proverbs influenced your conclusions.

SHARE YOUR EXPERIENCE

1. Think of a common proverb from your culture. Translate it into English, and write it on a slip of paper.
2. When you finish, give the slip of paper to your teacher.
3. When your teacher collects all the proverbs, he or she will give one to each student.
4. Taking turns, each student will then read the proverb and guess which culture it is from.

TALK IT OVER

1. Discuss the significance of these proverbs in their cultures. In what situations could each proverb be used? What does it mean to the members of the culture?
2. What insight into cultural values does each proverb give? What does the proverb say about the people who use it?

LEARNING STRATEGY

Testing Hypotheses: Gauge your understanding of the role of proverbs by interviewing.

OBSERVATION TASK

Interviewing about Proverbs

Ask an informant who is a native of your contact culture the following questions:

1. What three proverbs do people often use and believe in?
2. What does each proverb mean? What kind of thinking or behavior is the proverb encouraging?

Write their answers on the lines below:

PROVERB	VALUE
1. _____	_____
2. _____	_____
3. _____	_____

TALK IT OVER

1. What proverbs did your class collect?
2. What proverbs were given by more than one informant?
3. What values did the informants think the proverbs represented?
4. Have you come across any of the same values in your previous examinations of your contact culture? In what behaviors have you seen these values indicated?

HINT: Think about the observations, interviews and analyses you have done throughout this book as you answer the last question.

The heartbeat of a culture lies in its traditions and literature. Through channels like folk tales, poetry, songs, celebrations, and oaths a culture transfers its values among its members and down through the generations.

READING

"Cats in the Cradle," by Harry Chapin, is a classic song from the 1970s. It describes the relationship between a father and his son. As you read the lyrics or listen to the music, think about the message this song conveys.

Cats in the Cradle
by Harry Chapin

My child arrived just the other day,
He came into the world in the usual way.
But there were planes to catch and bills to pay,
He learned to walk while I was away.
And he was talking 'fore I knew it,
And as he grew, he'd say,
"I'm going to be like you, Dad.
You know I'm going to be like you."

And the cat's in the cradle and a silver spoon
Little boy blue and the man in the moon.
"When are you coming home, Dad?"
"I don't know when.
But we'll get together then, son.
You know we'll have a good time then."

Well my son turned ten just the other day.
He said, "Thanks for the ball, Dad. Come on, let's play.
Can you teach me to throw?"
I said, "Not today. I've got a lot to do."
He said, "That's okay."
And then he walked away but his smile never dimmed
And said, "I'm going to be like him, yeah.
You know, I'm going to be like him."

And the cat's in the cradle and a silver spoon
Little boy blue and the man in the moon.
"When are you coming home, Dad?"
"I don't know when.
But we'll get together then, son.
You know we'll have a good time then."

Well, he came from college just the other day,
So much like a man I just had to say,
"Son, I'm proud of you.
Can you sit for a while?"
He shook his head and he said with a smile,
"What I'd really like, Dad, is to borrow the car keys.
See you later,
Can I have them, please?"

And the cat's in the cradle and a silver spoon
Little boy blue and the man in the moon.
"When are you coming home, Son?"
"I don't know when.
But we'll get together then, Dad.
You know we'll have a good time then."

Well, I've long since retired, my son's moved away
I called him up just the other day.
I said, "I'd like to see you,
If you don't mind."
He said, "I'd love to, Dad, if I can find the time.
You see, my new job's a hassle and the kids have the flu.
But it's sure nice talking to you, Dad.
It's been sure nice talking to you."

And as he hung up the phone,
It occurred to me.
He'd grown up just like me.
My boy was just like me.

And the cat's in the cradle and a silver spoon
Little boy blue and the man in the moon.
"When are you coming home, Son?"
"I don't know when.
But we'll get together then, Dad.
We're going to have a good time then."

Published by Story Songs Ltd. ASCAP

TALK IT OVER

1. How would you describe the stages of this father-and-son relationship?
2. How do you think the father's feelings changed over the years?
3. What cultural values about family relationships or child-rearing can you infer? Identify the lyrics from which you infer those values.
4. What does the song say about the importance of work to these men?

OBSERVATION TASK

Collecting Song Lyrics
1. Find a song or poem from your contact culture that you feel represents a prominent cultural value.
2. Bring it to class and share it with your classmates. Discuss the cultural values that your song reflects.

LEARNING STRATEGY

Personalizing: Teach your classmates about your culture by sharing songs and other cultural artifacts from your culture.

SHARE YOUR EXPERIENCE

Think of a song or a poem in your native language that expresses an important cultural value. Share it with your classmates, either by singing it, reciting it, or playing it from a tape. Discuss the cultural values the song or poem reflects.

READING

With your teacher, discuss the following questions before you look at the Boy Scout Oath. These questions should help you get a sense of the role of the Boy Scout Organization in U.S. culture.

1. What is a Boy Scout?
2. What is the purpose of this organization? How long has it existed?
3. Approximately how many boys do you think have participated in this organization over the years?
4. Who knows and says the Boy Scout Oath?

The Boy Scout Oath
"On my honor I will do my best to do my duty to God and my country and to obey the Scout Law; to help other people at all times; to keep myself physically strong, mentally awake, and morally straight."

Threads

The Boy Scout's Motto is "Be Prepared."

CONTRIBUTE YOUR IDEAS

1. In groups of three or four, read the Boy Scout Oath aloud at least twice. Clarify the basic meaning of words and phrases you are not sure of. Ask each other first. If that fails, ask your teacher. Be sure you know the meaning of "on my honor," "do my duty," "Scout Law," "mentally awake," and "morally straight."

2. Analyze this Oath, trying to discover the morals, values, and beliefs that are conveyed through its words. Remember that this Oath has been taken by all Scouts since the beginning of the organization.

HINT: For your analysis:

a. Look at each phrase individually.
b. Talk about its possible meaning to a boy.
c. Discuss the responsibilities a boy accepts when saying this phrase.
d. Name the values and beliefs this phrase assumes the Boy Scout holds.
e. Record your thoughts.

TALK IT OVER

As a class, discuss the values that you think the Boy Scout Oath represents.

11.4 CULTURAL VALUES—OBSERVING AND INTERVIEWING

As you have done throughout this book, you can now turn to the members of your contact culture who themselves may be able to tell you their values. You can obtain their views by observing them and by interviewing them.

OBSERVATION TASK

Behaviors in a Shopping Mall

As a class, or in large groups, go to a shopping mall to observe the people and their behaviors for evidence of the values they hold. Begin your observation with a quick walk through the mall, using the BEHAVIOR model to gather some basic information. As you observe, notice that evidence of values appears in many different forms.

After your initial walk through the mall, discuss with your classmates the forms in which evidence of values appeared. To understand these values better, you next need to study one form in depth. Decide which students will study which forms and what methods you will use. You may wish to consider the following forms: the advertising seen in the stores, the styles of dress modeled in the windows, the speech of the salesclerks, the talk of the shoppers in the dressing rooms, or the activities other than shopping that people engage in. Other forms to focus on include who shops together, how many people shop in one group, how the shoppers are dressed, and differences in the ways people of different ages and genders shop.

Take notes on what you see. Remember that you are trying to discover something about the values of the people in the mall, so observe carefully and write down your observations, not your opinions.

TALK IT OVER

Discuss your findings. What new evidence do you have of the values that structure your contact culture?

Personal Values

Until now, you have been investigating cultural values. Individuals also have personal values that may or may not reflect the general values of their native culture. It is time now for you to consider the individual and the influence of these personal values on his or her behavior.

CONDUCT AN INTERVIEW

Conduct an interview with a member of your contact culture. Preferably this person should be at least 25 years old. The purpose of this interview is to find out from members of the culture what their personal values are. As you have probably discovered in your analysis of your own culture, it is not always easy to identify one's own values. Sometimes we haven't thought about them or put a name to them. Nevertheless, we all act according to the values we hold. This is often particularly clear when we are making value judgements on other people's behaviors. The following questions are designed to help you and your informant identify his or her values. You may wish to tape record your interview. If you do not record, be sure to take good notes. Ask your informant to clarify anything you do not understand.

Interview Questions
1. How would you describe a "good" person? What qualities make someone "good"?
2. What qualities do you admire in a person?
3. How would you try to raise your child? What attitudes, beliefs, or values would you try to teach him or her? Can you give some examples of ways you might try to teach these things?
4. What qualities do you least admire in a person? What characteristics upset you or make you angry?
5. When you evaluate someone as a marriage partner, what are you looking for?
6. What do you think a person's role in society is? What duties to society do they have and not have?
7. What quality best serves a person throughout his or her life?
8. Where should a person's first loyalties lie? With self? Family? Friends? Government? Religion? Somewhere else?
9. Name one song that you like. Do you think it reflects any of your personal values?
10. Can you think of an oath, promise, or similar type of statement you have made that reflects your personal values?

JOURNAL

Reviewing Your Journey

What insights have you gained about cultural values? Combining these insights with those you have gained throughout the book, how well do you understand the values of your contact culture? What questions have you been able to answer? What questions do you still have?

THE JOURNEY CONTINUES

From observing behavior to inferring values, your cross-cultural research skills have been sharpened. Learning about culture is more than knowing trivial facts and customs; it involves understanding the intricate ways in which worldview and behavior interact. Now you are better equipped to travel further in exploring culture, understanding people, and, as a result, better understanding yourself.

Chapter 12 concludes this book by giving you a chance to identify your own preferences regarding methods of culture learning. It encourages you to continue down the road of culture learning using the observation skills you have acquired and guided by your own goals and directions.

Your Journey Continues

Walk tenderly in the first snowfall. Later on you can shovel and storm and cuss and bemoan. But the first snow is like a newborn baby—so clean and soft, it makes the world newborn. Walk gently into that first snow.

–Kim Williams

INTRODUCTION

"We have learned that one can acquire roots and flourish in places where others have lived by trying to understand and respect their lives."

–James Oliver Robertson and Janet C. Robertson,
All Our Yesterdays

Throughout this text, you have walked in the footsteps, been to the places, talked to the people, spoken the language, and read and heard the media of your contact culture. If it has been your goal, you have also acquired roots and flourished. Journeys are exciting. Each experience takes in new sights, new information, new ideas. As you remember your journey, you reflect on what you have done and learned and how you have changed. As you think back, you also look ahead to what you would like to do next time, what else you can learn, how you may still change. It is time now in this journey to pause and consider where you have been and where you would like to go next. These two paths will form the focus of this chapter.

12.1 WHERE YOU HAVE BEEN

READING

A Culturgram

A "Culturgram" is a newsletter published by Brigham Young University. Each Culturgram presents facts about a different culture. Read the Culturgram about Russia on the following pages and think about the type of information it includes.

CULTURGRAM '94

Russia
(Russian Federation)

Franz Joseph Land

Novaya Zemlya

Kara Sea

Barents Sea

Laptev Sea

East Siberian Sea

Murmansk

Siberia

Lena River

Nizhniy Novgorod

Ob River

Yenisey River

Kasan • Sverdlovsk

Angara River

Magadan

St. Petersburg

MOSCOW

Sea of Okhotsk

Voronezh

Volga River

Lake Baikal

Amur River

Vladivostok

Boundary representations not necessarily authoritative.

CUSTOMS AND COURTESIES

Greetings

When meeting, Russians shake hands firmly and might say *Zdravstvuyte* (pronounced sdrav-STVUH-teh, it means "Hello"), *Dobry dien* (Good day), or *Privet* (Hello). Some women prefer not to shake hands, but it is impolite for a man not to offer his hand. Friends and family may kiss on the cheek. The question, "How are you?" (*Kak dela?*) is taken literally; Russians answer in detail and at length. Asking the question without waiting for a full response is rude. *Kak dela?* is not used as a formal greeting. Titles such as Mr. (*Gospodin*) and Mrs. (*Gospozha*) were not used under the Communists, but they are slowly being revived. In addressing an older or respected person, one uses the given name and a patronymic (possessive of father's first name), but surnames are preferred in formal greetings.

Visiting

Russians like to visit and have guests. Sitting around the kitchen table and talking for hours is a favorite pastime. Shoes are sometimes removed after entering a home. Refreshments are usually offered, but guests may decline them. Friends and family may visit anytime without prior arrangement. They make themselves at home and can usually expect to be welcomed for any length of time. Visits with new acquaintances are more formal.

Giving gifts is a strong tradition in Russia, and almost every event (birthdays, weddings, holidays, etc.) is accom-panied by presents. For casual visits, it is common (but not required) for guests to bring a simple gift (flowers, food, vodka) to their hosts. What is given is less important than the friendship expressed by the act. Flowers are given in odd numbers; even number are for funerals. If a bottle of vodka (which means "little water") is opened, custom dictates it be emptied by those present.

Eating

Eating with the fork in the left hand and the knife in the right is standard, but many people use only a fork. Hands are kept above the table and not in the lap. Most Russians like to eat a large breakfast whenever possible. Soup is common for lunch or dinner. Traditionally, a popular feature of any meal is *zakuski* (appetizers). There are many different kinds of *zakuski*; eating too many may spoil an appetite. Russians put more food than they can eat on the table and leave some on the plate to indicate there is abundance (whether true or not) in the house. Guests who leave food on the plate indicate they have eaten well.

Russians generally don't go to lunch in cafes or restaurants because the few that exist are fairly expensive. Instead, people eat at cafeterias where they work or bring food from home.

Gestures

Pointing with the index finger is improper but commonly practiced. It is impolite to talk (especially to an older person) with one's hands in the pockets or arms folded across the chest.

EURASIA

THE PEOPLE
General Attitudes

Russia's long history of totalitarianism has made fatalism a vital tool for survival. The inhabitants of Russia have had few opportunities to make their own decisions, whether ruled by a Czar or the Communist party. Personal initiative, responsibility for oneself, and the desire to work independently were suppressed by the state, and one was expected to conform to official opinion and behavior.

Now that communism has been dismantled, Russians are searching for new social values. The resulting confusion and chaos have led some to wonder whether the old ways weren't better. Many Russians are not happy with their rapidly changing society, which is characterized by inflation, severe shortages of food and other goods, unemployment, and a greatly reduced quality of life. They are not certain they are prepared to pay such a high price for economic freedom or wait so long for the benefits of a free market to become apparent. Others are eager to take advantage of the new environment.

Although proud of their accomplishments, Russians are basically pessimistic and usually don't express much hope for a better life in the future (except among the youth). Even a generally happy and optimistic Russian might not show his true feelings in public, but rather express frustration with everyday life. Friendship is extremely important in Russia. Russians are open with and trusting of their friends, and they rely on their network of friends to supply food, clothing, and other hard-to-find goods.

Russians, used to obeying the government without argument, are learning the value of discussion and compromise, of personal creativity, and of taking risks. This process will take some time and may only be realized with the younger generation. When *perestroika* (restructuring) began in the late 1980s, urban society became so highly politicized that by 1991 thousands of people were participating in public demonstrations. Soon, however, people became frustrated with the pace of reforms and felt they were not really impacting the decision-making process. With everyday life getting harder, most people stopped political participation and concentrated on making ends meet.

Personal Appearance

Russian clothing styles are the same as in Europe, but not as sophisticated. Jeans are popular among most age groups. In winter, people wear fur hats (*ushanki*). Shorts are becoming popular among the younger generations. The older generation dresses conservatively.

Population

The population of Russia is about 149.5 million. There are some 120 different ethnic groups, but most are small. Ethnic Russians form 82 percent of the entire population. Other groups include Tartars (4 percent), Ukrainians (3 percent), Belorussians (less than 1 percent), Udmurts, Kazakhs, and others. The capital and largest city is Moscow, with a population of over 10 million. Other large cities (one to three million residents each) include St. Petersburg, Sverdlovsk, Voronezh, Kasan, and Nizhniy Novgorod. Most Russians still live in rural areas, but there is a clear trend for young people to move to the cities.

Language

Russian is the official language in the country, and it was also the main language of the Soviet Union. Russian uses the Cyrillic alphabet, which consists of 33 letters, many of them unlike any letter in the Roman (Latin) alphabet. Non-Russians also speak their own languages. For example, Tartars speak Tartar, Chuvashes speak Chuvash, and Udmurts speak Udmurt. These individual languages are taught at schools only in each republic (state) of Russia where the ethnic group is prominent. Non-Russians are bilingual because they speak Russian in addition to their native language. However, they often consider Russian a second language and do not speak it on a daily basis. For their part, ethnic Russians are not required to study other local languages. Foreign language courses are limited, but English, French, German, and Spanish are offered in schools.

Religion

The Russian Orthodox church is the dominant religion. After the October Revolution (1917), the Communists separated the church from the state (which were previously tightly bonded) and began to discourage all religious worship. Many churches were forced to close under Lenin and Stalin. Mikhail Gorbachev was the first Soviet leader to change official policy and tolerate—even support—religion. Yeltsin has also embraced the church, which is regaining its political influence. There are almost only Russian Orthodox churches in rural areas, but nearly every major religion and many Christian churches have members in large cities. Islam is practiced in many southern regions.

LIFE-STYLE
The Family

The family is the basic social unit in Russia and most people expect to marry and have a family. The average urban couple has one child, but rural families are larger. Because housing is difficult to obtain, young couples often live with their parents for some time. It is the normal practice to financially support children until they reach adulthood. The father is considered head of the family. Both husband and wife usually work, but women are also responsible for housekeeping. Men rarely share in household duties. Child care is available, but few families can afford it. When the elderly live with their children, they often provide child care and do the shopping.

Urban apartments are very small, and it is common for a family of three or more to live in one room. A typical apartment has one room, a kitchen, and a bathroom. Rural homes are small, but larger than apartments. While they have more room, they often lack running water.

Dating and Marriage

When young people date, they usually go to movies or for a walk in a city park. Sometimes they go to bars or cafes, but this is presently too expensive for most people. Instead, the youth like to have parties in their apartments when their parents are not home. Premarital sex is common, as is living together before or instead of marriage. There is a new trend to be married in a church first and then to have an official civil ceremony in a "wedding palace." Wedding palaces were the only places people could get married before 1991.

Diet

Although food is plentiful, many products are very expensive or can only be found in hard currency markets. For the common person, this means fruits and vegetables are hard to come by. Hence, their menu consists mainly of bread, meat, and potatoes. Those on fixed and limited incomes (mainly the elderly) eat more bread than anything else. Common Russian foods include *borsch* (cabbage soup with beets), *pirozhki* (a stuffed roll), and *blini* (pancakes) with black caviar. *Borsch* is still one of the most popular foods in the country. Its ingredients (potatoes, cabbages, carrots, beets, and onions) almost complete the list of vegetables used in everyday life. Pork, sausage, chicken, and cheeses are popular, but they are often very expensive. Russians prefer tea to coffee. Mineral water, juice, and soda are readily available at high prices. Russians drink far more vodka than wine.

Business

The business week is 40 hours, with Saturdays and Sundays off. Offices are generally open from 9:00 A.M. to 6:00 P.M. They close at lunchtime (1:00 P.M.). Prices in state stores are not negotiable, but prices on the streets, where an increasing number of items are being sold, are flexible. Capitalism is booming in Russia, and a new generation of entrepreneurs is beginning to thrive. Numerous small businesses and joint ventures with foreign firms are finding success, and employees of state-run factories are buying them and working hard to make them profitable.

Under communism, there were no incentives for bureaucrats to perform well or to even be nice to clients, so the usual answer to any question was "no." This practice is still found in society, but "no" is no longer not final. One must simply bargain and be persistent to get what one wants. Russians prefer to have social interaction before discussing business. Trying to do business on the phone without seeing the prospective business partner is ineffective. One spends a lot of time in meetings before even a small deal can go through.

Recreation

Russians have little leisure time because of the hours they must devote to getting food, working extra jobs, or taking care of their households. Urban Russians spend their spare time at their *dachas* (country cottages), if they have them, relaxing and growing fruits and vegetables for the winter. There are really no nightclubs, and entertainment usually ends by 11:00 P.M. Even Moscow is essentially dark and quiet after that.

The Russians' favorite sport is soccer. Sports in general, but particularly winter sports such as ice skating, hockey, and cross-country skiing, are popular in Russia. Watching television is the most common way to spend extra time. Gathering mushrooms is a favorite summer activity. Theaters and movies are highly appreciated, but they are only available in big cities. Rural people can watch movies at *dvorets kultury* (palaces of culture), which serve as community recreation centers.

Holidays

New Year's Day is considered the most popular holiday in Russia. Almost everyone decorates fir trees and has parties to celebrate the new year. Grandfather Frost leaves presents for children to find on New year's Day. Christmas is on 7 January, according to the Julian calendar used by the Russian Orthodox Church. Women's Day is 8 March. Solidarity Day (1 May, also known as May Day) is a day for parades. Before 1991, people were required to attend; now they do it voluntarily and the nature of the celebrations has changed dramatically. Victory Day (9 May) commemorates the end of World War II and is especially important to the older generation. Easter and Christmas observances, long interrupted by communism, regained their prominence in 1990.

THE NATION

Land and Climate

Russia is the largest of the 15 former Soviet republics and the largest country in the world. At 6,592,734 square miles (17,075,200 square kilometers), it is nearly twice the size of the United States. Russia is bounded by the Arctic Ocean in the north, by the Pacific Ocean in the east, and in the south and west by many countries. Four of the world's largest rivers (Lena, Ob, Volga, and Yenisey) and the world's deepest freshwater lake (Baikal) are in Russia. Most of the country's territory consists of great plains, but there is a large tundra in the extreme north, and much of western Russia is covered by forests. Parts of eastern Russia are desert. The low Ural mountains divide Russia in two parts: the smaller European and the larger Asian regions. The climate is generally dry and continental, with long, subzero winters and short, temperate summers.

History

Slavic peoples settled in eastern Europe during the early Christian era. In 988, they were converted to Christianity by Prince Vladimir. At the beginning of the 12th century, the area was conquered by the Mongols, who dominated the Slavs for 240 years. In 1380, the Slavs defeated the Mongols and regained their sovereignty. Ivan the Terrible (1533–84) was the first Russian ruler actually crowned Czar of Russia. He expanded Russia's territory, as did Peter the Great (1682–1724) and Catherine the Great (1762–96). The empire reached from Warsaw in the west to Vladivostok in the east. In 1812, Russian troops defeated France's Napoleon, and Russia took its place as one of the most powerful states on earth.

When Czar Nicholas II abdicated because of popular unrest during World War I, Vladimir Lenin, head of the Bolshevik party, led the 1917 revolt that brought down the provisional government and put the Communists in power. Lenin disbanded the legislature and banned all other political parties. A civil war between Lenin's Red Army and the White Army lasted until 1921, with Lenin victorious.

In 1922, the Bolsheviks formed the Union of Soviet Socialist Republics (USSR) and forcibly incorporated Armenia, Azerbaijan, Georgia, Ukraine, and Belarus into the union. During Lenin's rule, which ended with his death in 1924, many died as a result of his radical restructuring of society. Lenin was followed by Joseph Stalin, a dictator who forced industrialization and collective agriculture on the people. Millions died in labor camps and from starvation. At the start of World War II, Stalin signed a nonaggression pact with Hitler, but Hitler soon invaded (1941) the Soviet Union, and the war eventually took over 25 million Soviet lives.

Nikita Khruschev, who took over after Stalin's death in 1953, declared he would build real communism within 20 years, but his reforms and policy of *détente* with the West were opposed by hard-liners and he was replaced by Leonid Brezhnev in 1964. Brezhnev orchestrated the expansion of Soviet influence in the developing world and ordered the invasion of Afghanistan. Brezhnev died in 1982 and was followed by two short-lived leaders, Chernenko and Andropov.

After emerging as the new leader of the Soviet Union, Gorbachev started *perestroika* in 1986. He attempted to reform the system by introducing *glasnost* (openness) and new freedoms, such as freedom of speech. He promised to allow privatization and free enterprise, but many reforms failed. An unsuccessful coup in August 1991 exposed inherent weaknesses in the Soviet system, and the country quickly unraveled. Russia, led by its elected president, Boris Yeltsin, became an independent country and moved to introduce democratic and free-market reforms.

Often challenged by hard-liners, Yeltsin found it difficult to pass reform legislation. In 1993, he received public support through a referendum on the future course of Russia's government. He subsequently convened a constitutional assembly to draft a new constitution. Congressional opponents tried but failed to stop him. Elections for a new parliament and president were planned for late 1993 upon finalization of the constitution.

Government

If constitutional reform succeeds, a president subordinate to the Congress of People's Deputies will be replaced by a strong executive president. The Congress and its standing parliament (Supreme Soviet) will be replaced by a two-chamber federal assembly: the Council of Federation will include representatives from Russia's 89 regions and republics, and the State Duma's members will be elected according to like-sized districts. In addition, greater autonomy will be granted to local governments.

Economy

Russia's natural resources give it great potential for economic growth and development. Natural gas, coal, gold, oil, diamonds, copper, silver, and lead are all abundant. Heavy industry dominates the economy, although the agricultural sector is potentially strong. Russia's economy is weak because of past Communist policies and the current disruption of production and distribution. In 1992, Yeltsin launched radical reforms designed to liberalize prices, attract foreign investment, and privatize the economy. Prices skyrocketed. Many reforms will take time to succeed, but privatization is taking hold and seeing some success. Unfortunately, while Russia clearly intends to establish a free market, few people have even a modest knowledge of how it should work. The currency is the *ruble* (R).

Education

Education is free and compulsory between ages six and seventeen. The literacy rate is 99 percent. There are over two hundred universities, medical schools, and technical academies. Graduates are required to take government-assigned jobs for at least two years.

Transportation and Communication

Most people use public transportation. Major cities have subways, trolleys, and buses. Taxis are expensive and hard to find, but unofficial taxis are increasingly common. *Aeroflot*, the national airline, provides domestic and international air travel, but it is unreliable. Railroads are extensive, but the system's service is poor. The telephone system is old and inadequate. The press is free, active, and constantly changing. Thousands of new publications have come and gone since 1990.

Health

Medical care is free, but the quality of service is poor. Doctors are highly trained and qualified, but they lack modern equipment and medicine to adequately treat their patients. The infant mortality rate is 31 per 1,000. Life expectancy ranges from 63 to 74 years. Common major diseases are alcoholism, cancer, diabetes, and heart ailments.

For the Traveler

U.S. travelers are required to have a valid visa and passport to enter Russia. Visas are also necessary to visit individual cities. Vaccinations are not required, but some may be recommended. Check with your local health authority before traveling. Drinking water is generally safe, but bottled water is recommended. Take plenty of film, as it can be difficult to find in the country. There are many opportunities to experience the Russian culture through travel; contact your travel agent for more information. You may also wish to contact the Russian Embassy, 1825 Phelps Place, NW, Washington, DC 20008.

TALK IT OVER

1. Who might benefit from the information in the *Culturgram*?
2. What part of the *Culturgram* did you find most interesting?
3. On a scale of 1–5, how would you rate the *Culturgram* in terms of providing helpful information?

very helpful				not helpful
1	2	3	4	5

4. On a scale of 1–5, how would you rate the *Culturgram* in terms of providing important information?

very important				not important
1	2	3	4	5

5. Why did you choose these scores?

Creating a *Culturgram*

The tasks you have completed and the materials you have worked with throughout Journeys *have introduced you to "culture" somewhat differently than it is presented in the Culturgram. What you have learned about culture and about cultural investigation has prepared you to create a description of your contact culture from both observational and participatory perspectives. You have increased your expertise and are ready to share it with those who can benefit from your knowledge and experience.*

CHOOSE TOPICS AND WRITE A CULTURGRAM

1. With your classmates, list on the blackboard the categories of cultural information (or topics) you believe should be included in a *Culturgram*.
2. Individually, decide which of these topics you would most like to develop as your part of the *Culturgram* and join with those classmates who choose the same topic. If you are writing a section of the *Culturgram* related to one of the chapters in this text, review that chapter and the results of your various activities. You may wish to look at other projects and activities that you and your classmates have done earlier.
3. Then, write your section.

DISTRIBUTE *CULTURGRAMS*

Combine the sections written by all of your classmates into a single *Culturgram*. Make a copy for each member of your class.

Finally, think about who can benefit from your *Culturgram*. Would other students in your school, members of your community, or friends in your home country value this information about your contact culture? Make copies available to these individuals.

12.2 WHERE YOU WOULD LIKE TO GO

CONSIDER THIS

What would you still like to learn about your contact culture? What will help you carry out this learning?

_____

_____

_____

_____

_____

_____

_____

_____

_____

_____

Creating Tasks for Further Culture Learning

The activities you have participated in throughout Journeys *have been composed of two primary and, often, a third complementary component. The primary components are the* **topic,** *or content, of the activity and the* **type of task** *used to complete the activity. The third component is the* **learning strategy** *used while you engaged in the activity. As you know, strategies have not been listed for every task but have been selectively identified to acquaint you with various task-strategy combinations. From your experiences with this text, you will become aware of your own preferred learning strategies for performing various tasks.*

IDENTIFY PREFERRED TOPICS OF INVESTIGATION

Review the content of *Journeys*. Look at the chapter titles and scan the topics covered in each chapter.

Then, read the list of topics below and think about which ones you enjoyed the most. Put a check next to those topics you would like to investigate further.

_____   Cultural Awareness

_____   Cultural Adjustment

_____   Worldview

_____   Places

_____   People

_____   Social Institutions

_____   Language and Communication

_____   Media

_____   Values

_____   Other: _____

IDENTIFY TASK TYPE PREFERENCES

Review the activities you have engaged in throughout *Journeys*. Which tasks did you enjoy? Which tasks did you not enjoy? Check the tasks below that you would like to engage in again. Also, check the group types, the language skills, and the cultural focus you prefer.

TASKS	GROUP TYPE	SKILLS	CULTURAL FOCUS
_____ Observing	_____ Individual	_____ Speaking	_____ Sharing your native culture
_____ Interviewing	_____ Pair work	_____ Listening	
_____ Discussing	_____ Small group	_____ Writing	_____ Investigating your contact culture
_____ Reporting	_____ Whole class	_____ Reading	
_____ Drawing pictures			_____ Learning about your classmates' cultures
_____ Dramatizing			
_____ Conducting research			
_____ Listening			
_____ Reading opinions			
_____ Inferring			
_____ Interpreting charts			
_____ Thinking about issues			
_____ Sharing your experiences			
_____ Contributing your ideas			
_____ Stating your opinions			
_____ Focusing on language			

IDENTIFY LEARNING STRATEGY PREFERENCES

Throughout this text, strategies have been labeled with one of the seven names below. Study the following list, which summarizes these categories.

Managing Your Learning

These strategies help you take control of and responsibility for your learning. Throughout *Journeys,* management strategies involve you in:

- planning and preparation for your observations and interviews.
- separating tasks into steps.
- organizing your findings.
- summarizing in preparation for review.

Testing Hypotheses

These strategies lead you to verify your expectations and interpretations as you are learning. In *Journeys,* hypothesis testing strategies involve you in:

- listening to your classmates' opinions.
- comparing your expectations to the findings of your observations.
- interviewing cultural informants.
- interviewing native speakers.

Forming Concepts

These strategies help you identify the most meaningful elements of what you are learning. In *Journeys,* concept formation strategies involve you in:

- categorizing data.
- forming opinions and ideas.
- evaluating statistical information.
- comparing new concepts to familiar ones.
- seeing relationships among individuals.
- reading charts and interpreting data.
- analyzing physical materials.
- inferring function and value.
- drawing conclusions.
- abstracting key points when reading.

Remembering New Material

These strategies help you retain what you have learned. In *Journeys,* memory strategies encourage you to:

- demonstrate what you have learned.
- write down questions you want to ask informants.
- record interviews on tape and in written notes.
- review information in preparation to applying it.
- associate English and your contact culture with your native language and native culture.
- express new information in proverbs, acronyms, poems, and songs.

Overcoming Limits

These strategies help you find new ways to gather cultural information. In *Journeys,* strategies for overcoming limits ask you to:

- increase your knowledge through observing.
- increase your knowledge through interviewing.
- increase your communication skills by becoming aware of specialized language.
- use context to fill in missing information and appropriate meaning.
- read research related to the subject of your observations.

Personalizing

Personalization strategies allow you to experience the personal component of culture learning. In *Journeys,* these strategies ask you to:

- view a culture through its members' eyes.
- understand yourself as a way to understand others.
- see your contact culture as a member of the culture would.
- link your feelings to the feelings of others.
- share advice.
- link your native and contact cultures.

Understanding and Using Emotions

These strategies help you realize the emotional component of culture learning. In *Journeys,* emotional strategies lead you to:

- consider your feelings.
- consider others' feelings.
- view the role of humor in expressing feelings, views, and social reality.
- express viewpoints and emotions through language and pictures.

After becoming familiar with the list, rank the strategy categories by writing the number 1 next to your most favored strategy or strategies, number 2 next to your next most favored, and so on until you have marked your least favored strategy with the highest number.

____	Managing Your Learning	____	Remembering New Material
____	Testing Hypotheses	____	Overcoming Limits
____	Forming Concepts	____	Personalizing
		____	Understanding and Using Emotions

CREATE CULTURE LEARNING TASKS

Create tasks you would like to engage in as part of your continued culture learning. As you compose your tasks, follow the format used throughout this text. Consider the task topic and the task type (and the group type, language skills, and cultural focus). Also, identify the learning strategy or strategies to be used. Your tasks may be related to one another, or they may focus on different issues. You may want to create a task using the BEHAVIOR model.

Evaluate Your Tasks

Ask a classmate to read and comment on the tasks you have created:

1. Have you chosen appropriate tasks for the subjects you want to investigate?
2. Have you identified appropriate strategies for the tasks?
3. Revise your tasks if necessary, following your classmate's suggestions.

Engage in Your Tasks

Complete the tasks you have created.

Report Your Findings

In small groups, report your findings.

12.3 REFLECTING ON WHAT YOU HAVE LEARNED

JOURNAL

Reviewing Your Journey

Evaluate the tasks you created. Did they allow you to gather the information you wanted? Did they increase your understanding? Did you choose the task types and strategies that best help you learn about your contact culture? Do you feel you can now study culture on your own?

THE JOURNEY CONTINUES

This chapter has asked you to synthesize your knowledge of your contact culture in the form of a Culturgram. It has also encouraged you to initiate further cultural investigation. Your cultural learning will not stop with this book, nor does it end with your current contact culture. The interests and skills you have developed may be used as you continue to investigate your contact culture, as you discover other cultures, and even as you consider your native culture.

Your cultural knowledge has increased since you first began observing the people in your life. As long as there are people around you and as long as you choose to learn from them, your cultural journey will continue.

"It is the lesson of anthropology that intercultural communication is difficult. But given the motivation . . . a significant level of mutual understanding is possible."

–Alma Gottleib, *Parallel Worlds*

Appendices

OBSERVATION QUESTIONS

Individuals:	Whom do you see?
Background:	Where are they? What objects and materials are also present?
Activities:	What are they doing?
Expressions:	What are they saying?
Order:	What happened before this behavior began? What will happen next? How long have they been there? How long will they remain?
Rules:	What must individuals do to participate appropriately in this behavior?
Hopes:	What is the purpose of the behavior? What do the individuals want to accomplish?
Values:	Why is this behavior important? What does it reveal about the individuals and their culture?

OBSERVATION CHECKLIST

_____ Did I receive permission, if permission is necessary, to observe?

_____ Did I prepare for the observation? Did I think about what I might see and hear? For example:

    _____ Where will I observe this behavior?

    _____ What activities do I expect to see?

    _____ Whom do I expect to see?

    _____ What do I expect them to say?

    _____ What do I expect to be their reasons for participating in this behavior?

_____ Am I at the observation site a few minutes before I am to begin my observation? Did I bring several sheets of paper and a good pen?

_____ Am I sitting or standing in a place where I can observe, but not interfere with, all activities?

_____ Am I taking notes on everything I observe?

_____ Am I observing both what is happening and how it is happening?

_____ Am I writing down just the things I see happening?

_____ Am I recording enough evidence to support any assumptions or inferences I will be making?